Glow
in the dark

Charles Stock

Glow
in the dark

living in God's
creative energy &
supernatural joy

DESTINY IMAGE® PUBLISHERS, INC.
P.O. Box 310, Shippensburg, PA 17257-0310
"Speaking to the Purposes of God for This Generation and for the Generations to Come."

This book and all other Destiny Image, Revival Press, MercyPlace, Fresh Bread, Destiny Image Fiction, and Treasure House books are available at Christian bookstores and distributors worldwide.

For a U.S. bookstore nearest you, call 1-800-722-6774.
For more information on foreign distributors, call 717-532-3040.
Reach us on the Internet: www.destinyimage.com.

Trade paper ISBN 13: 978-0-7684-3234-3
Hardcover ISBN 13: 978-0-7684-3422-4
Large Print ISBN 13: 978-0-7684-3423-1
Ebook ISBN 13: 978-0-7684-9063-3

For Worldwide Distribution, Printed in the U.S.A.
1 2 3 4 5 6 7 8 9 10 11 / 13 12 11 10

Dedication

I dedicate this book to all the seekers who feel the inner thirst for the Rivers of Eden. Don't stop. There really is much more there than we can imagine....

Acknowledgments

I started this journey with Anne more than 40 years ago. We came to Jesus at the same time and entered in with our whole lives. She gave me children who've given me grandchildren. She made this journey with me and generously gave me time and encouragement to live, to explore, and to write. Thank you, Anne, for believing with me and in me. You shine!

Thank you to the amazing staff and loving people of Life Center, who have welcomed the Holy Spirit, embraced our Father, and participated in a radiant culture of love, worship, and creativity that won't fit in a box!

Endorsements

Few authors can blend brilliant thinking and the journey of genuine spirituality like Charles. Just one quote from his book says it all: "You are a container filled with the Age to Come and carrying the Future of All Things! If we really grasp this, we live in holy awe, as stewards and as portals into the heavenly realm." Charles is one of those rare gifts in the Body of Christ who can take you through a portal of insight and bring you back to earth with a fresh perspective that permanently changes the way you live.

Dr. Lance Wallnau
Lance Learning

Did you know that the presence of God is infectious and contagious? You can be a shining light in the midst of a dark world! My friends Charles and Anne Stock live their lives filled with the radiant, joyful presence of the Holy Spirit. You too can arise and let your light shine for the glory of God. But watch out—the contents of this book might just make you dangerous to others around you and empower you to such an extent that you will never ever be able to live another boring day the rest of your life. Let His shining presence fill you!

James W. Goll
Founder of Encounters Network and Prayer Storm
Author of *The Seer, Dream Language,*
The Lost Art of Intercession, and many others

Glow in the Dark is a compelling, persuasive, profound, practical, and strategic treatise that invites us to be fully immersed in God's awesome presence. My dear friend Charles Stock has elegantly laid out a blueprint for the Presence-driven believer who desires to maintain intimacy with the Father, Papa God, in every moment of his or her life. Each chapter beckons us to understand progressively how to live present to God, present to ourselves, and present to the moment. With remarkable insight, clarity, and simplicity, Charles gives us the tools we need to live in God and have God live in us in the twenty-first century in such a way that our consciousness is expanded to realize who we are and what we carry wherever we go. Once you start reading this life-long learning manual on being Presence-driven, you won't be able to stop!

Dr. Mark Chironna
The Master's Touch International Church, Orlando, Florida
Mark Chironna Ministries

Charles makes me hungry. It seems every time I talk with him, my appetite is stirred for more of Jesus. This book will stir you, too. Every story is bursting with the joy of unfolding love-adventures with the Lover of our souls. Charles' innovative presentation of glimpses into the heart of God will fill you with wonder. I laughed. Cried. And smiled. My soul plunged into fresh places of His amazing kindness. Charles and Anne truly "live in love" and "live to love." You, too, will be drawn to join them in deep pools of the love of God.

Dave Hess
Senior Pastor, Christ Community Church, Camp Hill, Pennsylvania
Author of *Hope Beyond Reason*

Charles Stock challenges and reshapes our idea of normal Christianity. His book, *Glow in the Dark,* reveals that each of us is created to continually enjoy the Father's pleasure and live as vessels of love, fully possessed and overflowing with Glory. We are all called to be so united with Jesus that His very nature shines from within us as an irresistible light in this dark world. I am thrilled to be able to recommend this book that gives us keys to bearing exponential fruit, all year round! Charles is just amazing! He is a dear friend and it is a great privilege to recommend this awesome book.

Heidi Baker, PhD
Founding Director, Iris Ministries, Inc.

We were created to reflect God's character on the earth and thus to transform the world around us. *Glow in the Dark* draws the reader into a journey of discovering the profound commission of having our countenance and our very lives filled with the fullness of God. Charles' testimony of searching for and discovering truth paints a clear picture of coming out of darkness into marvelous light. Charles is a deep thinker, whose sanctified intelligence God has used to forge a way into the mysteries we need to comprehend in the days ahead. His book stirs a hunger for encounters and speaks to the heart cry to be filled and possessed with the presence of God. Once filled with His presence, we have a life-changing effect on the world around us. *Glow in the Dark* is sure to encourage and challenge the reader to pursue the "more" that God has promised.

Bill Johnson
Pastor, Bethel Church, Redding, California
Author of *When Heaven Invades Earth* and *Face to Face*

Contents

Foreword

When Moses came down from Mount Sinai carrying
the two Tablets of The Testimony, **he didn't know**
that the skin of his face glowed because he had been
speaking with God (Exodus 34:29 MSG).

"He didn't know." The emphasis is mine and not Mr. Peterson's (the translator of *The Message* Bible). When Charles told me the title of his book, I playfully suggested that it might be called *Glow in the Daytime.* This book is not really a how-to-do-it manual as much as it is a mandate for authentic New Testament Christianity. I once heard a Bible teacher refer to the historic moment in Moses' life when he *"wist not that the skin of his face shone"* (KJV). He then remarked, I think cynically, "If you think it's shining, then it's not!" His intimation seemed to say that you too shouldn't know until someone tells you.

Sadly, many believers have bought into this concept that to believe one's face is shining is either the height of arrogance or a woeful absence of modesty. Neither a candle nor a light bulb has a sense of self-awareness, but Christians are called to function as "unconscious competents." We may not know that our shadows heal until someone points it out to us. However we do need to know that at some point an observation ought to be made that we *have been with Jesus"* (see Acts 4:13). I think believers often struggle between two poles of being either a sinner or a saint. When Paul tells us that he is "chief" of sinners, and yet acknowledges the residents of each New Testament community as "saints," it becomes important to distinguish between *our capacity* to do wrong and *our identity* as joint-heirs with Christ.

Glow in the Dark is a mandate manual that answers the question raised by the Ethiopian eunuch who responded to Philip's inquiry, *"Do you understand what you are reading?"* and he responded, *"How can I, unless someone explains it to me?"* (Acts 8:30-31). I believe a biblical humility enables me to embrace what the Father has called me to be and to do without either guilt or false modesty. We are, in fact, "God containers"! Greater is He who is *in* you. Paul tells us, *"And you are in Him, made full and having come to fullness of life [in Christ, you too are filled with the Godhead—Father, Son and Holy Spirit...]"* (Colossians 2:10 AMP).

Charles and Anne Stock are pioneers who dared to explore, to go into the Promised Land and bring back irrefutable evidences of the reality of the Father's promise. Like Abraham who said, "God caused me to wander," they have found something that vindicates the questions of the timid, the skepticisms of the cynical, and the delight of those of like-precious faith who dared to go with them. They are "river guides" of the first order, and you can trust their assessment of what's in store for those who would dare to believe that risk of failure is the price of glorious success.

The principles shared in this book are tested and proven in various settings of life and ministry. There is an incredible church in Harrisburg, Pennsylvania, where the constituents are fluent in the language of the Presence and the atmosphere in their worship assembly is pregnant with a myriad of possibilities. Whoever you are and wherever you are on your faith journey, join the many who have discovered the joy of truly *glowing in the dark*. An exciting adventure awaits you.

Bishop Joseph L. Garlington Sr.
Senior Pastor, Covenant Church of Pittsburgh
Presiding Bishop,
Reconciliation! Ministries International

Introduction

Boundless Life Moment by Moment

Just about everyone is looking for "life!" Not just existence, but real living. And real living is laced with joy. If you haven't noticed, just take time out and observe some children. Even in circumstances that trouble many adults, kids tend toward happiness and play.

Tendency Toward Joy

Before we begin, I will confess that I am prejudiced. I lean toward optimism and fully believe that it's good to be alive! If that's not enough, Jesus declared clearly that His purpose in coming was that we might possess an excessively superior quality of life, one that drips with the joy of Heaven (see John 10:10 MSG).

Born smack in the middle of the baby boom, I grew up in a resort town three hours east of San Francisco, in the Sierra Nevada. Catering to recreation and vacationers was a key industry in this area. During the summer months, the population would swell from 1,500 to 10,000. When the skiing was good, the winter weekends and school holidays would also bring hordes of skiers and other snow enthusiasts. Even the opening weekends of deer season and trout season brought a swell of visitors to our small, picturesque town in the pines. As a community, we were focused on hospitality, and specifically that people were having a good time. During winters that were warmer or drier than usual, businesses that counted on the tourist trade would put up signs calling on those driving by to "Pray for Snow!" When there was plenty of snow, some of these same signs read, "Don't Eat Yellow Snow!" In order to prosper, we needed legions of happy skiers and tobogganers to come, enjoy themselves, and spend their money. I can see that this focus on fun shaped my outlook on life and developed a value system that had high regard for joy and pleasurable activity.

Our home was less than a block from the local golf course and two blocks from the small lake that was the center of summer daytime activities. Behind our home was a small mountain with hundreds of acres of wild woods. My mother taught first grade but was home during the summer. She regularly shooed my four brothers and me out of the house, which no doubt gave her some peace, but also gave us a major dose of fresh air and sunshine. In the winter, we were only about 15 miles from a popular ski resort. Our home was not spiritually active, nor was it particularly happy, but through regular interaction with the vacationers around us I learned that life could be full of fun and joy.

Perhaps it was my developmental experiences, or it could be a God-given propensity, but my adult life has been characterized by a joyful pursuit of His Kingdom and His righteousness. In that, I have found more joy than words can convey.

After almost 40 years since I met Jesus, I am still in love with Him. Just about every day of my life, my heart traces its way back to the wonder of the New Life He freely gave me and keeps giving me! This simple practice keeps me from getting overly opinionated and critical of those around me. Keeping it simple hasn't been simple, but it has definitely been worth it! Marriage, parenting, and now grandparenting all have their demands and rewards! I never wanted to be a professional minister. I wanted to be a Jesus person. I still do. And I remain a Jesus person, undeterred by over 30 years of what most would call professional ministry.

My wife, Anne, and I are blessed to inspire, serve, lead, and shape a creative community of wonderful young or young-at-heart human beings who are in love with Jesus. We are surrounded by a thriving, happy group of exceptional and ordinary, creative and humble believers who are demonstrating the powerful love of God. We are in the import/export business. Love from Heaven is our main product. We have trained thousands who are effectively exporting heavenly love all across the world! And we do it personally as well. It has been our joy for years and years to take the Good News and the renewal of the Holy Spirit into many nations. We live to love. We live in love. It is good.

What you are about to read could be a cure for religious misery and mediocrity. This abundant life we can live is the master work of all of God's wisdom and creativity. He has lavished upon us the best Heaven has to give!

The traps that keep so many frustrated, worried, bound by resentments, and bored are as common as they are destructive. The keys that unlock the prison are simple and easily applied.

You were created to be free!

You were created to live a life that is characterized by loving relationships, an abundance of possibilities, and fullness of joy. No matter how miserable your life has been to this point, you can move into a life that overflows with joy! Some of the happiest people I know came from the most wretched backgrounds imaginable!

The Benefits of Joy

Anyone in their right mind likes to be happy. Joy is pure pleasure. Laughter in particular is good for us. Studies have shown that in early childhood it is normal to laugh over 300 times each day. Not just smile, but laugh! Much of the laughter in children is unprovoked. They will giggle or laugh for no apparent reason. It just wells up from within. The health benefits of laughter include strengthening the immune system, reducing the craving for food, and increasing one's tolerance for pain. Joy and laughter help people heal more quickly.

By the time people reach 30 or 40 years of age, many have lost their laughter—on average laughing only about 15 times each day. The capacity for spontaneous joy seems to be one of the healthy marks of childhood and a positive aspect of childlikeness.[1]

Given the choice, children gravitate toward an activity that is fun. *The New Oxford American Dictionary* defines fun as "enjoyment, amusement, or lighthearted pleasure."[2] Yes! Simple fun is one of the deep wellsprings of *life.* The capacity to enter into enjoyment and lighthearted pleasure is a mark, not just of childlikeness, but of true wisdom and maturity.

It is pleasant to be around the pulsating energy of a person who is really engaged in living. Conversely, many are shriveled up and consumed by the toxic negativity that pervades the everyday lives of too many.

Joy is not only pleasant to the joyful, it radiates infectiously. It is mind-altering. Joy adjusts the way we see and the way we feel. When greeted by someone with a genuine smile and a twinkle in the eye, we can hardly keep from returning the smile. A lively anticipation springs up and before we know it, a party could break out! Small or large, celebrations of joy connect with a deep root in our humanness. When the pure energy of joy gets strong enough, it is really hard to be a grump. For those who know God, pleasantness is actually a preview of coming attractions. We've actually been summoned—not to appear before a dour judge, but to join the festivities of a supernaturally energized party! (See Hebrews 12:22.)

This is more than frivolity. Joy and celebration are the serious business of Heaven! It's a great gathering of "an innumerable company of angels" *and* the spirits of righteous men made perfect! (See Hebrews 12:23.) Can you imagine the noise, the shouting, and the jumping up and down in this glorious and raucous event? It's like all the Super Bowl victory parties, all the end-of-war celebrations throughout history rolled into one! It's way beyond "glad"!

And *this* is the starting point, the journey, and the destination. The reward for faithfully stewarding our God-given gifts is summed up in this: *"Come and share your master's happiness!"* (Matt. 25:21).

Yet most individual experience falls way short of overflowing joy and pleasure. Pain prevails over pleasure and despair over joy in countless lives. How do we get to this party on Mount Zion?

This book is written with the intention of helping you do what is humanly impossible. It is written as a guidebook to supernatural, grace-filled positivity! I'm not sure if everyone who reads it will glow in the dark, but I am convinced that some will. And if you don't actually glow in the dark physically, at the very least your countenance, your words, and your days will be filled with ever-increasing light. That's the life we are called to live.

Infinite Void of Darkness

> *God spoke: "Let us make human beings in Our image, make them reflecting Our nature…"* (Genesis 1:26 MSG).

Humans are created to live within the availability of infinite and benevolent pure energy. When humankind turns away from the love of God, he is the most dangerous species in the universe.

The morning was sunny and pleasant. Elizabeth, my daughter, was enjoying the breeze from her windows and open balcony door, engrossed in a homemaking project. Late April was green, and in the Denver suburbs, that was a distinct joy.

At 11:19 there were some small popping sounds, as if some firecrackers had gone off. She barely noticed the sound, focused on the work before her. She was unaware that directly across Bowles Avenue, a strange evil had been unleashed. Eric Harris and Dylan Kiebold had opened fire, killing Rachel Scott and wounding her friend Richard

Castaldo as they ate their lunches on a knoll next to the west entrance to Columbine High School.

Around 11:30, Elizabeth thought she heard lawnmowers, surprised that someone would be mowing so early in the spring. What she heard was not the sound of gardeners mowing, but of police helicopters responding to the unfolding nightmare. Bowles Avenue was closed for three hours.

Within minutes the military personnel, SWAT teams, other law enforcement, and emergency crews, converged to contain a yet undetermined peril. They fanned out, looking for additional threats. For that moment, in that locale, America seemed under siege. The tension stayed high until 3:00 P.M. when the authorities found the bodies of the shooters and determined that beyond these two middle class teenage boys there had been no other perpetrators. Littleton, Colorado, would be the focus of national and international attention over the next few weeks, as a stunned community grappled with a pointless massacre that resulted in 14 dead and 24 wounded.

Tragedies indelibly mark our lives. I was sitting in an eighth grade classroom when Mr. McDonald stepped into the hallway. He returned ashen faced, walked slowly to the front of the room, and with a broken voice told us that President John F. Kennedy had been shot. For America, it marked an end of an era of naive optimism.

Anne and I were running late on a Tuesday morning in September. We should have already been on our way to a regional pastors' retreat. A few minutes before 9:00 A.M. our phone rang. Our younger daughter was urgent in her words: we needed to turn on the television. Her husband worked in the Chrysler Building in midtown Manhattan. He was preparing to leave for a 10:00 A.M. appointment on the 103rd floor of World Trade Center 1. On his way out, he had just seen a big cloud of smoke rising from downtown and called to let her know.

We were soon captivated by the streaming news reports. It was still not clear what had just happened at the World Trade Center, but the North Tower had suffered an apparent explosion. There were reports that it may have been a plane. Just after 9:00 we watched in horror as a second airliner crashed the South Tower. We happened to see it live.

Horrified at the unthinkable, I turned to Anne and said, "Things will never be the same." For the thousands who died and for the tens of thousands who lost family and friends that day, this was even more true. It was instantly clear that something intentional and very evil was occurring. It was a "Pearl Harbor" event.

September 11, 2001, changed our world. Far, far worse things have happened all through history. Genocides. Deportations. Mass starvation. Great calamities are not unique in history, but they are eruptions of a deep internal magma within the collective soul of humanity.

Where does this dark hatred, this blind anger find its origin? Marred human nature reveals itself as lost in a maze, twisted by deception, a tortured distortion of the original Image. Pain, insatiable thirst, hopelessness, madness, and rage characterize the darker sides of human existence. Inside every son or daughter of Adam is a deep void, the result of the Fall.

Could human beings actually be the creatures through whom God actualizes His character on earth? Is it in and through *Homo sapiens* that the Creator of creation is perceived and revealed? What energizes such monstrous self-destruction?

The answers lie in the original design. Human beings are hardwired for worship, for connection with the Infinite. We were created for beauty, for delight, for walking with God in the cool, refreshing breezes of Eden. Full of joy, full of wisdom, full of love, the original pair knew only delight. The name of our original home was *Eden*. In Hebrew, *Eden* means "pleasure" or "delight." This Land of Pleasure was a protected paradise, full of every facet of delight.

> *Then God planted a garden in Eden.... He put the Man he had just made in it. God made all kinds of trees grow...beautiful to look at and good to eat....A river flows out of Eden to water the garden...* (Genesis 2:8-10 MSG).

Losing Our True Home

Paradise was our primordial habitat. There, pristine pleasures poured out into a River that gave vitality to human endeavor. Adam and Eve, the unproven prototypes, slaked their God-designed thirst for wonder and spirit from the living waters, which flowed sparkling and clear, straight from Pleasure. They strolled daily with the Creator in the pleasant evening breeze. How long our original parents lived in bliss is unknown.

What we do know is that there came deception, violation of trust, and incalculable loss. Humans lost their proper home. We now live as feral creatures, surviving and sometimes seeming to thrive, but lacking the original habitat of pleasure and daily friendship with Infinite Love. Human hearts ask in a million ways, "Does *Eden* really exist? Can I find my way home?"

Banished from Eden, the hardwired hunger for pleasure, for joyful, overwhelming intimacy with the Infinite remains. The need is there, but the capacity is warped. The God-breathed Scriptures declare that we are broken, dead in trespasses and sin. Inside every son or daughter of Adam is a deep and dangerous void, the result of the Fall.

> *Everybody dies in Adam; everybody comes alive in Christ*
> (1 Corinthians 15:22 MSG).

Destructive addictions, unbalanced obsessions, heroic pursuits, noble deeds of courage and sacrifice, cruel abuses, and more are common in history and unique to the human species. No other species displays such capacity for innovation and destruction. What is man? Is *Homo sapiens* truly wise? Are we only a sad shell of the original model?

As a race, we yearn for return to the River that flows from Pleasure to water the garden of life. Universally, water equates with life. The four headwaters of Eden beckon to us and yet frustrate our human desire to achieve and possess. How can we live without these waters of life? We search for the Fountain of Youth and the promise of eternal life. The history of individuals and cultures, nations and empires is written by the thirst for Living Waters poured forth from the Divine Nature.

Endnote

1. Kausalya Santhanam, "Laugh and Be Well," in the Sunday Magazine of The Hindu-India's National Newspaper (March 12, 2000).

2. *New Oxford American Dictionary, Second Edition* (London: Oxford University Press, 2005).

Looking for Eden

Human beings, godlike and infinite in potential, can either ruin or renovate planet Earth and even the entire Universe! Yet, we are born with darkened hearts and diminished comprehension of our personal mission and significance.

This is the story of my own journey, searching for meaning and true joy without a map or compass. I didn't have a clue why I was alive, but did have a sense that there was something out there that was bigger and better than anything in my immediate experience. And so I set out to find it. Since it is drawn mostly from memory, it is subjective and may not be the way someone else remembers it.

The times and the currents of culture defined the paths I traveled. Yet, I was drawn on by something pure and life-giving that was beyond time and culture.

By the joyful generosity of God I came to the True Light that lights up every human being. And there, I found a new beginning.

CHAPTER 1

Yearnings for More

I was the second of five brothers. For some reason, I was the only brown-haired boy in a family of blonds. We slept dormitory style in a big, finished attic. We loved the heavy snows that would come in the winter months. For us, they meant sledding, tobogganing, snowshoeing, and—when we got older—skiing!

Early memories of transcendence are rare for me. The Divine was not part of our family culture. But around the age of 13, a dormant thirst awoke within me.

Strangely alert in the middle of the night, I looked out from my second-story bedroom window, transfixed by pure wonder. The clouds had cleared and the full moon shone on a dreamscape of cedars and pines bowed like heavy candles under the weight of a foot or more of fresh snow. My heart raced. A part of my being touched the Beyond. Inside me, an inexpressible longing stirred. Something elusive beckoned me.

Looking in All the Wrong Places

What was this persistent sensation? Whispers of something otherworldly and beautiful came to me. Pop music is generally superficial, but all through the sixties, certain lyrics resonated with the hopeful emptiness in my soul. A certain kind of adolescent transcendence could be eked out of the Top 40 radio of the day.

The Seekers sang, *"There's a new world somewhere they call the promised land. And I'll be there someday if you could hold my hand...."* I felt it was so. I just didn't know who needed to hold my hand.

The Lovin' Spoonful asked, *"Do you believe in magic?"* Again, I did. Was it really *"in a young girl's heart"*? That seemed pretty uncertain. Maybe I could find that one who would be like *"sunshine on a cloudy day."*

Bob Dylan comforted and mystified me, calling out in raspy tones that *"the answer my friend is blowin' in the wind."* Was there actually something out there in the wind? Something beyond? Something unseen? If only it could be grasped and possessed.

I knew that *"The Times They Are a Changin'."* I was encouraged that *"the loser now will be later to win."* I just didn't know where to find that answer blowin' in the wind.

Open and searching, exposed to the ever-interesting, more urbane tourists who came to our little mountain town from the San Francisco Bay area, I was washed in many of the cultural currents of my day. The idealism of the Civil Rights Movement; the subtle politics, hedonism, and hopefulness laced through folk music; the rebellion and thinly veiled sexuality in rock music all hit home, filling my empty heart with conflicting messages and desires. I was a sitting duck for the sixties! Many escapes were available, but none led me where I longed to go. Hope for something better never left me. I was a *Daydream Believer*. Real love was *"an elusive butterfly."* I could never stop seeking. I had to find it.

Summers were particularly hazardous for the young seeker with a gigantic vacuum within, a propensity for adrenaline, and few clear boundaries. There was always a parade of temptations. In 1965, at the ripe age of 14, my friend Patrick and I regularly "borrowed" his dad's brand-new, high-powered Grand Prix and cruised the streets of our resort town looking for some "action." We did this while his parents were out socializing, usually several nights each week. This diversion ended suddenly one evening in a collision with a very large oak tree that destroyed the car. My only lasting injury was a front tooth that died upon impact with the steering wheel.

Pat's dad had been the Navy heavyweight boxing champion of the Pacific during World War II. When he arrived on the scene and asked me, "Why did you steal my car?" I was pretty frightened, focusing on his large clenched fist. Fortunately for me, when I told him that Pat had driven the car over to my house, he had a paradigm shift! So I didn't go to jail for grand theft auto, but this event changed my life.

Both Pat and I had to go to work to pay for the thousands of dollars in damages. We were both hired at Twain Harte Lodge, a local resort hotel, to work in the restaurant. This place became a big part of my life. It kept me out of a lot of trouble, since I usually had to work on Friday and Saturday nights. I worked there on and off for the next six years. The owners/managers really liked Pat and me. We did everything including, after a year or so, managing the place while they were gone for a few days. One of our more enjoyable—but definitely age-inappropriate—jobs was doing the inventory on the wine cellar!

Drunken Haze

Alcohol was the preferred social lubricant in those years. To fill the infinite void within, my friends and I came up with several systems that allowed us to steal all the liquor and beer we wanted. Lacking both supervision and self-control, we would regularly get drunk, sometimes to the point of oblivion. We frequently skipped our afternoon classes, hitchhiked, and walked to our stashes, and got blasted. By age 15, I had the characteristics of an alcoholic.

Of course, my grades slipped dramatically. Unfortunately—from my perspective—the report cards were mailed home at the end of my sophomore year. When my parents saw my nose-diving grades, I got in *big* trouble. But my addiction raged on. I hadn't hit bottom yet.

Sometime in the summer of 1966, Pat and I were at it again, planning to attend a teen dance at a nearby venue, the MiWuk Village swimming pool. As usual, we had some contraband liquor. In typical young male fashion, we had a competition to determine who could drink the most vodka straight. Unconcerned with any physiological consequences, I attempted to chug a fifth of vodka as fast as possible. I won the contest, thereby consuming a potentially lethal dose. As the ethanol had its effect, I became more and more incoherent, moving through the stages from charming drunk, to pathetic staggering fool, and then to falling and vomiting mess.

Pat, ever the ladies' man, parked me on the hood of a very nice Chevelle Malibu SS convertible while he went to look for beautiful young girls. Although I was incoherent, I remember that it had a beautiful metal flake blue paint job and white diamond tuck leather upholstery; it was obviously a trophy car. When Pat returned, he found me sitting next to a small pool of vomit, the gastric acid no doubt corroding the exquisite paint and lacquer. Clearly the owner would be furious. And it was likely he would be violent. We got out of there as fast as we could!

A few blocks away from the car hood, the root beer stand provided a place to stop. There, prior to passing out for good, I amused some friends by falling straight back onto my back and head with nothing to break the fall but the dirt and pine needles. I was feeling no pain. Finally, they dragged me out into the woods behind the place and left me to fate. I have a memory from this time of a really cute summer girl named Julie weeping over my semiconscious body. I was, in the truest sense of the word, wasted. By God's mercy, I didn't die, and I vomited enough of the alcohol to avoid brain damage (at least I hope). After a few hours my friends finally loaded me in the back of a station wagon and brought me home.

Our house was uphill from the street and by the time Pat and I made it up the 50 or so steps that led to our front deck, my parents were waiting. We were busted! In my stupor, I was puzzled over *how* my mom could tell I had been drinking! Disgusted at the drunken mess that stood before her, she took a swing to slap some sense into me. My mom had been a state champion softball pitcher, so fortunately for me, I collapsed on the floor at that exact moment. My mom's fingernail caught Pat on his lip, splitting it open. This turn of events defused my mom's anger into embarrassment that she had struck a seemingly innocent bystander! Compared to me, he seemed totally sober.

The next morning, I woke up still intoxicated. Evidently, my body was having a hard time processing so much alcohol. Sitting up, I declared to Pat, "Wow, this stuff is good. I'm still high."

He shook his head at me from the other bed and pronounced, "You are in *so much* trouble."

At that, the foggy memories of the previous night's exploits began to flood my pickled brain. Shortly after, my mom came upstairs, gave me a big piece of her mind, and informed me that I was grounded for basically the rest of my life other than going to work and to school.

Phantasmagoria and Altered States...

That incident signaled an abrupt end to my career as a teenage alcoholic. I swore off every form of alcohol and got on the wagon, devoting my junior year of high school to becoming a top rate intellectual. I was still looking for something real that would fill the empty place. I began to read existential philosophers, revolutionary political thinkers, and along the way was introduced to Eastern religions.

Meanwhile, I shot my mouth off complaining in French Three about the lack of cool candidates for student body president. An older girl who had more than enough of me retorted, "Well, if you're so smart, why don't you run?"

So I did. It turned out I had the bare minimal qualifications, having served in a couple minor offices in the ski club. Linda, my opponent, had served in everything, was super responsible, and exceptionally well qualified. Despite my total lack of commitment or any defined platform, my friends and I mounted a blitz propaganda campaign in the last week of the election, blanketing the school campus with colorful campaign posters that were as psychedelic as we could render them. We thought it was hilarious. I found my gift of spontaneous humor in front of the assembly right before the elections and wowed them with a made-up-on-the-spot platform of better food in the cafeteria, more hip radio stations on the PA system, and other shuck and jive. I won by a landslide. That's how the best man (or woman in this case) did *not* win. The campaign was fun, but the truth was that all my promises, like my heart, were empty ideas that sounded good for the moment but had no substance. After winning by a landslide, I had no idea what to do next. I think God put me in that position to save me from utter destruction during the next year.

A more obviously significant event occurred during the spring of 1967. As part of a world affairs group, I was sent as a delegate to the Model United Nations, held that year on the U.C. Berkeley campus. Suitably, my group represented North Vietnam!

During a break, I wandered down Telegraph Avenue, trying to soak up as much erudite wisdom as possible. In a bookstore named *Shambala* I came across a book written by former Stanford and Harvard professor Richard Alpert. The title was simply *LSD*. This book would profoundly affect my life. At Harvard, Alpert, along with Dr. Timothy Leary, Aldous Huxley, and others, was an early academic experimenter in the use of psychedelic drug therapy. He and Leary were dismissed from Harvard in 1963.[1]

Dr. Timothy Leary

In his book, Alpert communicated that if you took enough pure LSD you could understand the meaning of the universe and see God. That fueled my fire! Could this fill the void? Could this restore that indefinable lost paradise that beckoned me? I wanted to *see God,* the Ultimate Reality, the First Cause.

I set out on a mission to find pure, pharmaceutical grade $C_{20}H_{26}N_2O$, lysergic acid diethyl amide. No dope and no impure street drugs for me! I wanted to find God and not just get high! Dr. Alpert, who later changed his name to Ram Dass, would not be the last Jewish spiritual pioneer to influence my life.

Things were heating up in the Haight-Ashbury district, a three-hour drive or four-hour hitchhike from my home. The flower children were in bloom and Northern California was slip sliding into *the summer of love!* I was inspired by Scott McKenzie's song, *San Francisco.* I would go there every chance I could and try to meet some *"gentle people with flowers in their hair."* I was definitely *Groovin',* convinced that *All You Need Is Love.* Like millions of other American teenagers, I was looking for some baby to *Light My Fire!*

At this time, I had a Yamaha motorcycle and would occasionally dress up in elkskin moccasins and beaded gauntlets that my father had in a storage chest, trophies of living among the indigenous tribes of the Yukon Territory in the 1930s and 1940s. To these I added a bathrobe and a blue or red handkerchief folded and tied as a head-band. Thus attired, I would cruise the highways and back roads of my mountain town and its environs, heralding the dawn of the *Age of Aquarius.* Harmony and understanding seemed to fill my heart with ecstatic hope. Of course, I only did this in the gray light of summer dawn. My parents would have fainted if they had seen me!

By midsummer, I found my Holy Grail! John, my future brother-in-law, arranged for some pretty pure acid and we planned my first foray into the hallucinogenic world of LSD. That first trip was pretty overwhelming. I gazed upon multicolored wheels of burning light rotating in the night sky. Waves of intuitive knowing and psycho-spiritual chaos crashed over my mind. Standing on a mountain overlooking my hometown in the warm summer night, I felt like I was Adam. Although I didn't see Him, God seemed very near and I felt I was part of His cosmic greatness. This ecstatic state diminished in about six hours.

As we were "coming down," into sanity, John asked me if I wanted to live in that altered state and visit normalcy or vice versa. That was an exciting question to me. After a little thought, I said I wanted to live in the high.

What I didn't know was that this was a counterfeit of the real thing. It was a cheap thrill that opened a spiritual door to me, but it wasn't the real thing. Although I was feeling like I had found the Secret of the Universe, I was traveling a road of deception and pride that justified all kinds of double standards and situation ethics, including lying to the "straight people," those who didn't "know." I felt only the "enlightened" ones could know the truth. The others just couldn't handle it.

How I Began and Ended My First Mission

I was so enthusiastic about this new pseudo-enlightenment that I became an LSD missionary. Rather than sell the drugs for profits, I bought a blotter sheet with multiple hits (dissolved LSD was dropped on a sheet of blotter paper so that each "dot" was a dose) and proceeded to evangelize my high school, sharing the "good news" of better living through chemistry to those I deemed open to the new possibility. This underground missionary activity was rather dangerous for me, since I was also the student body president. Every day, first period, I sat at my desk in the office I shared with the guidance counselor, Mr. Talman. He was very nice and never seemed to suspect a thing.

However, my "converts" didn't follow my instructions and were soon dropping acid at the worst times, getting spaced out in class. Hmmm...back to the drawing board for me! What was really happening? My subjective conclusion was that the LSD removed the separation between fantasy and reality. If the underlying fantasy, the dream of the heart, was for peace and love, that's what tended to be experienced (bad trips excepted). But if the underlying desires and fantasies were more base, then all kinds of violent, lustful, or dark experiences might occur. LSD didn't really work as a sure fire way to know Ultimate Reality.

Not wanting to go to jail for such a hit-or-miss "way to God," I gave up being an LSD missionary. Clean from drugs, I deepened my immersion in Eastern philosophies and kept searching for truth in the radical politics of the New Left.

Wondering if I would find reality in the great halls of learning, I applied and was accepted at the University of California. I moved to Berkeley in the fall of 1968, with anticipation that there, in that unique intellectual and hip cultural milieu, I would find the Truth. Berkeley held many experiences in store for me, but enlightenment was not among them.

Endnote

1. Richard Alpert, Sidney Cohen, and Lawrence Schiller, LSD (New York: New American Library, 1966), p. 63 et al.

Berkeley in the Late 1960s

Approaching the university campus from the south, I would normally walk up Telegraph Avenue and cross Bancroft Way, entering Sproul Plaza. Chanting Hare Krishnas, dancers, artists, and musicians were often gathered there. Occasionally big rallies were held. I would notice all the photographers standing on top of the Student Union. Maybe they were FBI or journalists or both. All this was very interesting to me.

Holy Hubert

One of the very first times I walked on campus, I noticed a deeply freckled man standing and haranguing a small crowd. At first, I didn't know why this man was yelling. I realized he was some kind of religious fanatic. This was the first time I had ever seen a street preacher. He was very colorful, generally cajoling people with a mixture of hellfire and humor. His name was Hubert Lindsey, known among the students and hippies as "Holy Hubert."[1]

The more Hubert waxed passionate about the Gospel of Christ, the more it stirred up a thin young man with black, curly hair and a pointy goatee. This was "Isaac the satanist," who at times would stand hissing and mocking Hubert's oratory. Altogether, it was quite a dog and pony show. As I stood both intrigued and somewhat bemused by this street theater, Hubert wheeled about, pointing his finger straight at me, and declared, "And you, just look at you! You don't know what you're doing and you don't know what you're looking for! You need Jesus to wash your dirty little heart!"

I wasn't ready for that, and found myself feeling humiliated and a little bit uncovered by this outburst. After a few moments of acting as if

I hadn't heard him, I found a way to slink out of the crowd. After that, I kept my distance from Holy Hubert. Looking back, I see that it was probably the first prophetic word I had ever received in public! Perhaps it was the call of the Lord on my life. It was definitely a true word of the Lord, even if the delivery was pretty brutal!

Two Strikes and a "Peace" March

During my first year on campus, Berkeley was basically at war. There were three major controversies calling for general strikes of the student body. This was a pretty intense introduction into college life! Only about one month into the fall term, someone associated with the radicals set the auditorium of Wheeler Hall on fire, completely destroying it overnight. Its 90-year-old carved hardwood ceiling burned to ashes, a victim of the dispute demanding credit for a course taught by Eldridge Cleaver. I was shocked at this senseless destruction. It was the largest lecture hall on campus. Sociology 121x was an experimental course in which Mr. Cleaver promoted the violent overthrow of "the system." The students enrolled wanted full credit for the course. After all, even revolutionaries needed to keep their 2S full-time student draft status intact while they learned how to destroy the evil system. Otherwise they might end up in Vietnam!

The Winter Quarter was the occasion for various minority liberation groups to form an alliance into the Third World Liberation Front. I don't recall the specific demands, but I remember the chants, "On Strike! Shut it down!" I recall seeing a frail female Asian student brutally clubbed at Sather Gate as she attempted to get to class. The clubbing was delivered by a big black guy, who didn't seem like a student at all. After seeing that, I decided to scramble through the Strawberry Creek ravine to get the same destination. The San Francisco TACT squad was called in when things got really out of hand. They fought the protesters with tear gas, dogs, and clubs. It was the first time I had seen riot police up close and personal. I would keep my distance, but Hubert would be right there, defending the students from the police.

In April 1969, a huge antiwar march was organized. More than 50,000 marchers showed up on a Saturday, gathering near the marina in San Francisco. The marchers carried flowers, helium-filled balloons, and, of course, protest posters, which someone paid to have printed. (We never really asked who was bankrolling these affairs.) The march led up Van Ness Avenue and west on Lombard to the Presidio.

When we reached the Presidio, I was *shocked* to see a very angry speaker on the raised platform. He was a Latino Che Guevara-wannabe, complete with black beret. He was flanked on either side with very tough looking bodyguards, who were holding carbines and dressed in bandoliers full of ammunition! Who exactly were they planning to shoot? I thought this was an *anti-*war protest! Eventually we made it to Golden Gate Park, where most of crowd smoked dope and zoned out in the drizzle. This day added to my disenchantment with the New Left.

On my way back to Berkeley I concluded that the *Revolution Now* folks wanted to be in charge and to replace the existing government. Their role models were Guevara, Castro, Mao, and Ho Chi Minh! Mao wrote that political power comes out of the barrel of a gun. Lyndon Johnson and Richard Nixon seemed more rational than those guys!

People's Park

The culmination of this turbulent year came in the spring quarter. A vacant lot a block away from my dormitory was turned, almost overnight, into *People's Park*. The undeveloped lot was owned by the University. On two consecutive weekends, the "park" was quickly filled with flowers and brick paths and huge pots of soup being cooked to give away. Many of the addicts and panhandlers from Telegraph Avenue walked the two blocks to the Park to hang out there. It made Telegraph seem a little gentler and kinder. Maybe the Age of Aquarius was finally dawning!

However, the Park also created an opportunity for confrontation. That was the intended desire of those who paid for the sod and flowers. According to some radical commentators, the overnight park development was funded by the American Communist Party.[2] Political activist Abbie Hoffman saw it as a chance to "suck (Governor) Reagan into a fight."[3] My friends and I sure didn't know that. It just seemed like a wonderful place.

That is, until the Regents of the University wanted their property back. Imagine that! On Thursday, May 15, just before 5:00 A.M., I was awakened by a Paul Revere-type cry, "The pigs are coming! The pigs are coming!" Did I mention that the police were called "pigs" by many of us on the radical left? Not much love and good vibrations in *that* attitude!

Rushing into the street, I ran down to *People's Park* to behold a construction crew clearing a perimeter, drilling post holes, and erecting a 10-foot-high fence around the park. The construction crew was working behind a protective line of 250 California Highway Patrol officers. Feeling something free and beautiful was being unjustly murdered, I shook and wept. This was a great loss to vision for *"a new world somewhere."*

The students and counterculture community weren't going to take this sitting down! There was a rally at noon at the Sproul Hall steps attended by thousands. It was tense. The hippies were angry, the radicals wanted revenge, and even some students were spoiling for a fight. Dan Siegel, the student body president elect, took the microphone. During his speech he said, "Let's go down and take over the park."[4] The crowd began to chant, "Take the Park! We want the park!" Soon, a raging mass of indignant young folks poured off of Sproul Plaza whooping and shooting onto Telegraph Avenue to take back the Park. Sensing serious trouble, I chose to be an observer rather than a participant. I ran uphill, toward College Avenue. As I was running through Kroeber Hall, I looked out a window and saw a military helicopter whirring overhead. Below me in a secluded courtyard, a few hundred National Guard were *fixing bayonets* and *putting on gas masks!* Bayonets! This was very heavy.

It seemed the "parents" had anticipated the "tantrum." I was in shock. It felt like Vietnam had come to Berkeley! I scurried to College Avenue and across to Haste Street and made my way down Haste toward the Park. About that time, the mob was rounding the corner from Telegraph and coming up Haste. As I made my way down the street, I was uphill from the focus of the fight and able to be an observer. The CHP were firing tear gas canisters into the mob. The students hurled back stones, bottles, and pipes. I witnessed a "freedom fighter" pick up a live tear gas canister with his bare hands to throw it back at the police. Later I learned that when detonating, a tear gas canister can reach temperatures up to 400°F. Tough on the hands!

Meanwhile, near my dormitory two large school buses with blacked-out windows pulled up and out poured what appeared to be large, fat men in baby blue coveralls with full face mask helmets and clubs. These were the Alameda County deputy sheriffs. They were poorly trained, ill-led, undisciplined, and mean.[5] They were in identical jumpsuits with no badge numbers or other ways to identify them. Little better than thugs, they were armed and on the rampage. Later, the sheriff of Alameda County was fired for what occurred. But on that day, these guys, who hated hippies, students, and the counterculture, were totally unaccountable. We called them the Blue Meanies, and for good reason!

Students at Telegraph & Haste hurling stones at police. Fence posts visible behind police.

Right in front of me stood a slight young Asian student with an expensive single-lens reflex 35 mm Pentax camera, intent on capturing some history. He didn't see it coming. A Blue Meanie hit the young man's camera with a big billy club, shattering it on the concrete. When the young man looked down at his ruined camera, the officer whacked him on the neck with his club, and the student sprawled face down on the sidewalk. The officer continued on his mission to find troublemakers and subdue them.

Many brutal things happened that day in May 1969 and over the next few days. A young father, an artist, was blinded by birdshot that hit his eyes. Another man, watching from a rooftop, was killed by buckshot. The CHP and the Berkeley Police were restrained and professional, but the Alameda deputy sheriffs were *out of control!* Local radio station KPFA set up airwave propaganda. Many living in the neighborhood of Park tuned in and placed their speakers in the windows of their apartments. Buffalo Springfield's *For What It's Worth* offered an almost eerie commentary on the events.

> Something's happening here
> What it is ain't exactly clear
> There's a man with a gun over there
> Tellin' me I got to beware…

KPFA reached John Lennon by phone. He had been banned from the U.S. by the Nixon administration but was in Montreal with Yoko Ono at a peace demonstration. Lennon urged the protesters to organize a festival and chant "Hare Krishna." In a later call he explained, "The monster doesn't care. The Blue Meanie is insane."[6]

Not just radicals were affected. My roommate, Dan, was in the Naval ROTC and had been assigned to guard the computer center. In those days, computers were huge machines that ate and spit out punch cards. Those gargantuan computers needed their own buildings! Dan was a real clean-cut guy who had a military crew cut. He definitely was not easily mistaken for a hippie. On his way back to our dorm, he caught some birdshot in the back! It really, really upset him!

Students and National Guard with fixed bayonets near Student Union.

Another friend, Mark, who was legally blind with partial, uncorrectable sight made a wrong turn walking back to the student co-op where he lived. He was shot with double-ought buckshot through the calf. If it had hit the bone, his leg would have been shattered. If it had hit a vital organ, well…he wouldn't have been around to tell me about it.

Good Karma

The year 1969 was very disenchanting for a young idealist who thought that knowledge and countercultural ideals could produce a better world and lasting peace. The violence seemed to peak during the week preceding Memorial Day (I will describe this further in Chapter 13). I also noticed that the violence was random. The rioters didn't just attack the Bank of America (a favorite target) and other giants of the military-industrial complex, they ruined lots of mom-and-pop businesses. I knew this wasn't the way to enlightenment.

Basically giving up on *The Revolution,* I devoted myself to Eastern religions and finding peace within. I went to Kundalini Yoga classes as often as I could and tried to have good karma.

To make sure I had good karma, I told my parents not to send me any more money. If they knew what they were paying for, they wouldn't have liked it! This noble act caused my socioeconomic status to drop to about a half step above a homeless person for my remaining years at Berkeley. I was in reality a starving student.

I finished my second year as an "underground man," an unregistered occupant in a student housing cooperative. For my third year, I lived outside, on the balcony of some friends' apartment. For this "sublet," I regularly cleaned the apartment. I also worked part time as a carpenter's helper and did some landscape gardening for rich folks in the Oakland Hills. My mother had mercy on me and sent me $50 each month anyway. That probably kept me alive.

Endnotes

1. Dr. Hubert Lindsey, A.K.A. "RED LINDSEY" A.K.A. "Holy Hubert" (1914-?), born Georgia. His family, a prominent family with a Baptist background, later settled in Birmingham, Alabama. At the age of 13 years old, Hubert won the most freckled-face boy contest in Birmingham. It was from this point that he had his debut in the movie industry. Hubert was one of the original Little Rascals; playing the original cast of the Alfalfas.

   A successful theologian, church planter, and crusade preacher in the 1960s, Dr. Lindsey dissolved his large staff and went to

Berkeley as an unknown. For over three years Hubert spent eight hours a day preaching the gospel of Jesus Christ to social-ists, communists, Buddhists, Hindus, Marxists, Blasphemers, Atheists, and anarchists. Dr. Lindsey faced the crowds every day, ready to speak to every person.

In 1965 he arrived at Berkeley. He was beat up over 150 times in the first year for preaching Jesus outdoors on the campus. He stood face to face with people like Jerry Rubin, Eldridge Cleaver, Hell's Angels, Black Panthers, the S.D.S., the Manson family, hippies, and prostitutes and declared Jesus to them all.

"Holy Hubert" was notorious for running into a demonstration of thousands and taking away their microphone system, and preaching to the radicals. He would say things like, "Do you want a Revolution? I said, do you want a revolution? I can't hear you radicals, do you want a revolution?" By this time he would have all the hippies and socialists listening and would go on to say, "…You don't need a revolution on the outside. NO!!! You need one on the inside, and the greatest revolution you will ever have is when Jesus Christ, Son of the Living God comes into your hearts."

Dr. Billy Graham once asked Brother Lindsey, "Dr. Lindsey, what is the greatest demonstration that you have ever broken up?"

Dr. Lindsey replied, "35,000."

Billy Graham said "One man!?"

Hubert replied, "Jesus was with me, Dr. Graham!"

From YWAM Web site http://www.ywam.org.ph/.

2. David Horowitz, *Radical Son: A Generational Odyssey* (New York: The Free Press, 1997), 182-183.

3. Rob Kirkpatrick, *1969: The Year Everything Changed* (New York: Skyhorse Publishing, 2009), 100.

4. W. J. Rorabaugh, *Berkeley at War: The 1960s* (New York: Oxford University Press, 1989), 160.

5. Ibid., 117.

6. Ibid., 161.

The Mountains Beckon

By the summer of 1971, I had concluded that no one could find God in the chaos and controversy that regularly swirled through Berkeley. It was too distracting. For this reason, I returned to the mountains and got a job in the woods. I ate macrobiotic food, mostly brown rice, sesame salt, and mu tea, which I thought was particularly virtuous. After working all summer in the woods and buying a purple Volkswagen microbus, I had no desire to go back to Berkeley in the fall. So I kept working.

God was providentially guiding my life. He was arranging to slake my thirst. I was unaware of that, but felt like I should stay in the mountains if I ever hoped to attain the enlightenment I was seeking.

Meeting Anne

At the same time my future wife, Anne, was in Maine, working in a boutique in Old Orchard Beach. It was actually kind of a head shop and a front for some dealers in cannabis. In the fall she also returned to the Sierras to regroup and chill out. We were about to have a collision of destinies.

We had first met when we were both 14, in 1965. Every Wednesday night there was a teen dance at the outdoor roller rink in the center of our little downtown. Thousands of kids came from all over. Somehow, my friend Pat and I ended up in the line next to Anne and her friend, Judy, a Jewish girl from her school in San Francisco. Anne and her family were "regulars," meaning they owned a second home in our resort town and spent the whole summer, every summer. Her older brother and sister were Life Guards at Twain Harte Lake, which meant they were extra cool.

The previous summer a friend had pointed her out from a distance at the lake, and I thought she was the most beautiful girl I had ever seen. The next year, there we were, standing right next to her and her friend in line! I introduced myself and spent most of the night dancing with Judy, who had braces, a Jewish nose, and a hilarious sense of humor. I was too intimidated to directly pursue Anne.

After that, I deliberately made good friends with Anne's older brother, her younger brother, and her mother. I found any and every excuse to hang out at their house. In her eyes we were just friends. This went on for years. When I was 15 I told my friend Pat that I thought I would marry her. I don't know why I said that. She lived in San Francisco and only came up for the summer or in the winter to ski. Pat told me I was crazy. But, looking back, I can see that at the age of 15 God was whispering His destiny to me.

I never stopped thinking about her, but she always seemed beyond my reach. Most of my girlfriends reminded me of Anne in some way. Anne and I would spend lots of time talking and hanging out, but just as friends. A couple times during my first year at Berkeley, I borrowed a car and drove over to San Francisco to see her. I took her to a concert and we spent a day in Golden Gate Park. In the summer of 1969, I was in Twain Harte and she was living on kibbutzim in Israel (that was a hip thing to do). In the summer of 1970, she was in Twain Harte and I was hitchhiking across America.

In Love

But in the fall of 1971, Anne and I were both in the same place. We began to spend time together in October, and it soon became clear that we were in love! On my 21st birthday we spent hours sitting on the kitchen floor talking pretty much until dawn. It snowed about 5 inches that night, which was really unusual in October. It could have been a prophetic sign of all the potential that was involved in our connecting, for it would impact not just our own lives, but those of thousands and thousands in the years to come.

We spent that fall and winter reading *Autobiography of a Yogi*,[1] drinking mu tea, eating brown rice, and searching for spiritual truth. The author recommended that we pray, asking God to reveal our guru, or way, and our teacher, who would point to the way or guru. When we did this, Anne had a vision of Jesus. I told her that I thought it was just because she was an American and that we should keep searching. Too bad.

On the night of the Winter Solstice I proposed that if Anne and I were still together on the Summer Solstice, we should get married. Only a hippie would think this way, but six months later, that's what we did!

Still Seeking

Salvation by diet can be really tough. In February, we were on a ten-day cleansing fast, macrobiotic style, eating only brown rice and consuming hardly any fluids. We hitchhiked 11 miles in a snowstorm—and almost froze to death—just to buy some rice cakes!

In the early spring of 1972, I began working as a carpenter's apprentice and getting ready for my summer job as a river guide on the Stanislaus River. It was a very alive time for us. But in many ways, the emptiness was becoming more apparent. I had escaped the insanity of Berkeley. I was living in the mountains, eating macrobiotic foods, and practicing yoga. We made trips to Berkeley to buy organic foods and occasionally connected with a yoga ashram. I had connected with the girl of my dreams. For 21 years of age, it seemed I had it made.

But there was still an empty place in my inner being. I had not yet found the Rivers of Eden.

Endnote

1. Paramahansa Yogananda, *Autobiography of a Yogi* (New York: Philosophical Library, 1946).

The Karmic Path to Jesus

Looking for Pure Water and the Parable of a Dead Battery

In the summer of 1971, I was learning the art of rowing through the whitewater rapids on the Stanislaus River between Camp Nine and Parrott's Ferry. We used tough, inflatable boats made for professional river touring. Working as a river guide was a dream job. Warm weather, clear water, and stunning canyon scenery provided a daily feast to the senses. Some class IV rapids and an occasional emergency situation satisfied the need for an adrenaline rush.

Along with learning to row and mastering the river guide role, I discovered some of the sweetest water I had ever tasted flowing from springs in the limestone and basalt cliffs! Since I was a devotee of the natural high, I marked the locations of these springs for future reference and explored nearby areas for yet more.

Sometime in March or April of 1972, as Anne and I were pursuing enlightenment and salvation through diet and yoga, we made regular trips to a particular spring I had found that seemed the best of them all. We drove her old push-button transmission Dodge Lancer to a remote site. Getting to the water involved climbing through a barbed wire fence, crossing a pasture, and passing over a ridge into a small valley where a spring bubbled forth from pure limestone into a clear pool. An added benefit was the best watercress I had ever tasted growing at the lower end of the pool. We filled gallon glass jugs with water and cut as much watercress as we thought we could use.

As we headed back to the car, the clouds, which had been growing darker, let loose with heavy rain. This presented a problem to us. The alternator on the car wasn't working and the electric wipers were draining the already weak battery. It didn't seem we could make the 15-mile drive back up the mountain to Twain Harte. Our best bet was to visit our river guide buddies, Ken and Paula, who lived a couple miles away on top of Table Mountain, to recharge the battery. Pulling off the macadam onto the dirt road leading to their place, we climbed to the top of the small mountain. But when we arrived at their secluded home, we were disappointed. They weren't there. The rain had let up, but it was getting dark.

By this time, the battery was so dead that it wouldn't turn the engine over. I tried to restart on compression by driving recklessly as fast as I could down the twisting dirt road that led from their home. I never reached the required speed to restart the engine with the automatic transmission. I did almost get in a wreck! We found ourselves at the bottom of the mountain on Rawhide Road. Needless to say, we weren't happy hippies. Our flower child veneer was crumbling in frustration. In the distance we saw a light and decided to walk to it, hoping there might be a phone we could use to call a friend. It turned out to be a small church building.

Twelve Rednecks and Two Hippies

Arriving on foot at Table Mountain Chapel, we saw some cars parked in front and went to the door. We were met by a few middle-aged men, who seemed surprised to have two flower children show up at their meeting. Anne was wearing a purple paisley India print bedspread sewn into a dress. My bushy hair extended beyond my shoulders and I wore huarache sandals, hand cut from old tires. We smelled of patchouli and frangipani oils. Despite the fact that we were clearly hippies and they were real cowboys, they were very kind to us. We explained the situation and asked to use the phone. There was no phone but these men gladly offered to help us.

It happened that they were planning to begin a Bible study, and asked if we could wait until they finished or if we needed to hurry. Since it was against the rules for hippies to be in a hurry, we said we could stay.

The pastor, observing this group of older men with leathery, sun-beaten faces and real cowboy boots with two hippies added at the last minute, stated he felt impressed to review some earlier part of their study. They were studying First Corinthians. I didn't know what that meant, but I was about to find out! We were given a King James Bible to read along with them.

The pastor read a passage. We followed along. There were statements regarding the Cross, the power of God, and the wisdom of men. A couple of things really stood out to me.

> *For it is written: "I will destroy the wisdom of the wise; the intelligence of the intelligent I will frustrate." Where is the wise man? Where is the scholar? Where is the philosopher of this age? Has not God made foolish the wisdom of the world?*
> (1 Corinthians 1:19-20)

As he read, I was overwhelmed with a feeling that I had been, in the words of Spiro Agnew (Richard Nixon's Vice President), "an effete intellectual snob."

Could it be that all my pursuit of personal enlightenment was really in vain? I did my best to resist the feeling. I was seeking wisdom, but had not yet found it. Perhaps wisdom was not to be found in the normal way. What did it mean that the message of the Cross was foolishness? He read more than that, but I was transfixed, experiencing God knocking on the door of my heart in a new way.

After the Bible Study, which didn't last too long, the pastor and another man took the battery out of our car. They drove us and our dead battery to Scotty's Chevron station, just east of Sonora, California. They told us that Scotty was a "brother."

While our battery was being charged, they took us to someone's house and served hot milk with *Ovaltine*. While we were drinking they told us with great enthusiasm how many young people were coming to Jesus and being delivered of drugs. These were the years of the Jesus Movement. Tens of thousands of young people were finding Jesus as the Way to God. I thought that was great and told them how I knew some people that had really cut back on drugs and were now doing yoga or transcendental meditation. I don't think my response was what they were looking for.

In a while our battery was fully charged, and since we didn't have any money, the pastor cheerfully paid $2 to Scotty Chester. They seemed like very nice people. We all drove back out to Rawhide Road and reinstalled the now potent battery. I was really thankful and asked for their address so I could mail them the $2 they had spent. They laughed and said it was a gift, but I insisted. They suggested that we go to church and put the $2 in the offering. I said that I would. OK! We shook hands on it.

I now felt obligated to go to church in order to repay my debt. I kept remembering, too. I didn't want any bad karma to be assigned to my account.

Since I usually worked on the river on Sundays, I couldn't make it to a Sunday morning service, but I checked out a nearby church in Twain Harte and discovered they had a Sunday evening service. A week or so after the dead battery incident, on a Sunday night, Anne and I walked into the little Chapel in the Pines and went up to the front row, or perhaps the second. I had my $2 and was ready to make good on my pledge. I was totally unfamiliar with churches and the fact that two barefooted hippies in the front row would be a phenomenon, especially since this was my home town.

Looking back on this from the vantage point of over 30 years, I can see the hand of the Lord in the story. It was like a parable. We were going to great lengths to find crystal clear, pure water. With great effort we filled jugs with the waters of life. However, our vehicle wouldn't get the water home because the battery was dead and the charging system was broken. Along the way, we came across a homely outpost of Heaven—Table Mountain Chapel—and there we received unconditional acceptance and unearned kindness. We received this small gift with sincerity and appreciation and eventually it led us to the Ultimate Reality. But I don't want to get ahead of myself.

Drawn by the Presence

The Sunday night service we attended was a surprise to me! I went in order to place $2 in the offering. But God had a more significant purpose. The small congregation sang some hymns and devotional songs. The genre and quality of the music was not appealing, but that's not why we were there. Then the pastor, who everyone called Russ, announced that he felt like they should have a "testimony" service and invited the congregants to share significant personal encounters of a spiritual nature.

I don't know how many people got up and spoke, but it had an impact. Several of the older people shared visionary experiences in which they personally and mystically encountered *Jesus Christ!* They spoke with obvious authenticity and some with tears. I was stunned! Having spent the past five or six years pursuing an unknown God, I was amazed that there were spiritually alive people living right under my nose in my hometown.

How could it be that I had never known? The ones who spoke were of different ages: some like us, young people from the baby boom; some older; and many from my parent's generation!

These were the people I had tacitly dismissed as lacking spiritual insight. I assumed in my philosophical pride that people like this had nothing of consequence to share with me. From the first acid trip I took, I had closed my eyes to the wisdom that was around me, pursuing the psychedelic path until that proved pointless. After drugs, I cycled through Eastern philosophies, radical politics, occult dabbling, extreme diets, and more, caught in a maze of futility. I thought to myself, *I've taken drugs, eaten brown rice, and stood on my head for five years trying to find God. And these people seem to have known Him all along!*

The service ended with some kind of prayer. There was no offering that night.

As we walked across Cherokee Drive to our purple VW bus, Steve, who carried an obvious spiritual presence, approached us before we started the engine. I had known him distantly since I was about 10 years old. He was a year older than me, and the son of the pastor.

"Hey, you beautiful people, how are you?" he greeted us.

I wasn't used to being addressed in complimentary ways. I wondered why he said that. His manner was loving and sincere and he had a surprisingly strong personal magnetism. Steve encouraged us to come back on a Wednesday evening for a meeting with a group of younger people who he said were more like us. He said that Jesus was there and we would really enjoy the time.

For some reason, when Wednesday evening approached, it seemed like the right thing to do. So we went back to the little church. This was a new world for Anne and me, but everyone seemed very open and sincere, so it wasn't too uncomfortable. After a couple gospel songs that were corny to our taste, the sizable group of younger people was dismissed to the modest house next door.

About 70 or 80 crowded into an open living-dining room area, mostly late teens and people in their twenties, with one or two older than that. The format was simple. There were three accomplished guitarists who led us in folk-style spiritual songs that exalted God and Jesus. I enthusiastically threw myself into the worship of God. However, I was uncomfortable with songs that ascribed worship to Jesus. I considered Him a great teacher and holy man, but not actually God. Clearly those around us had no such reservations. Despite my reservations, I sensed a very pronounced and pleasant Presence as we began to sing. I welcomed this feeling as some kind of "natural high." These were *really* good vibes!

I liked being near the guitarists who were leading the singing. At times they sang beautiful and mystical songs in languages I had never heard. I assumed they were ancient Hebrew or Greek words, something like the Sanskrit mantras I learned in Eastern religions. Little did I know that these were words straight from the Holy Spirit! I got close and tried to sing the words. The Holy Spirit was drawing us to Jesus. We had no idea that we were being reeled in on the loving prayers of those who looked beyond our faults and saw our need.

Some pretty comical situations occurred in these first few weeks. On the second week, the leaders wanted two different groups who had joined together to meet each other. We were instructed to meet a couple people we hadn't met yet and to share our "testimony" concerning "how long we had known Jesus." I was a fairly adept people handler, so I deflected the questions with, "How long have *you* been saved?" or other similar questions that shifted the focus of the exchange. Most people were so happy to talk about themselves that they didn't notice, but one young woman would not be put off. She finally cornered me. I confessed to her that I thought I knew God but didn't see a need to "be saved" in the same way she did.

Almost instantly I was surrounded by "soul fishermen" trying to land a big one! If we had been near a door, we would have slipped out and never returned! Steve, who was leading the meeting, noticed our distress and called the group back into worship or some other focus. Phew! That was a close one.

A week later, the group decided to practice for the big Mother Lode Roundup Parade coming up on Mother's Day in nearby Sonora. The group marched in formation through the surrounding streets while singing praises to Jesus. We passed a house where some friends of mine were grilling steaks and drinking beer out on the deck. They were puzzled to see Anne and me in the midst of the group joyfully singing *Lift Jesus Higher!* When they hollered out to ask me what in the world I was doing in the middle of a bunch of Jesus Freaks, I just smiled and shrugged. Even with these awkward experiences, we kept coming back. By now, I had forgotten the $2 offering, instead drawn by the deep and tangible sensation of touching the Divine.

Finding "The Way"

After about three weeks or so of these meetings, I found myself alone in the house where I was staying. A few weeks earlier we had been in the Financial District in downtown San Francisco shopping for wedding rings. There in the noise of cable cars, streetcars, cabs, and buses, we heard some beautiful music. We followed it. It sounded like Peter, Paul, and Mary. It must have been a supernatural phenomenon, because when we traced it down, we found one guy with a 12-string guitar and another singing along with a tambourine. They had a guitar case open to collect money. It was nice music, but as I realized they were singing Christian songs, I began to get a little uncomfortable. Despite that, I found myself at the front of the small crowd that had gathered.

During a break, the two minstrels shared that the Lord had sent them to San Francisco on a mission. They had some Christian newspapers that they offered to the crowd for 25¢ each. I didn't have a quarter and was starting to leave, when one of the young men stopped me. He asked me if I would like one of the papers. I replied that I didn't have any change, but might return after we got some change at a store. He looked me in the eye and told me that he "felt the Lord wanted him to give me" the paper. He made me promise that I would read it. I took it, and since I was trying to store up good karma, I didn't throw it away. I put it on the toilet at my house. It sat there for at least a week. None of the articles were very interesting, but I wanted to keep my word.

About a week later, I looked through its pages again. I wanted to read at least one article and then throw it out. Buried in the middle pages of the paper, I found a short article with a title something like *Politics, Brown Rice, Yoga, and Jesus.* The title was provocative. I could read that! It was only a few paragraphs long, but it would be change the entire direction of my life.

It was a personal story of a man and his wife. It seemed like these people were my "cosmic twins," connected to me in an uncanny way. The couple had lived in the University District of Seattle seeking truth. Like me, they cycled through psychedelic drugs, revolutionary politics, and various Eastern mystics but concluded that the radical intensity of the University District made it too confusing to find ultimate reality. Looking for truth and sanity, they moved to the east slope of the Cascades and opened a macrobiotic restaurant in a small town.

Macrobiotics? Just like me.

Even more intriguing, they spent a few months reading *Autobiography of a Yogi*. They prayed the recommended prayer, for a guru and a teacher.

We had prayed this same prayer!

Shortly after they prayed this prayer, a young man started coming into their restaurant and ordering a bowl of brown rice, which he ate with chopsticks while reading a Bible. They were drawn to this man's peaceful spirit and would talk with him. Eventually, they recognized him as the teacher they had prayed for. He pointed them to the Way: Jesus!

The article went on to describe the changes that had taken place in their lives after connecting with God the Father through Jesus!

I was deeply affected. They had found what I was seeking.

At that moment, I recognized my prejudice against Jesus as Lord and Christianity in general. This was cultivated by teachers, authors, and professors, and fueled by my own pursuit of alternative routes to God. Could it be that I had rejected the Truth and the fullness of Life? It was time to sincerely offer my heart and mind to this Jesus of Nazareth.

Going out into the living room, and kneeling on a yoga mat, I carefully repeated the *sinner's prayer* included in the article. I had no idea how this worked, so I carefully spoke each word. I didn't feel any great sensation, but as I finished, I prayed what I believe was the commitment of my heart, "Jesus, if You will show me You are real, I will follow You with all that I am."

Amazingly, Anne, who was in San Francisco staying with her mom, prayed a very similar prayer during the same week. The following Sunday, we went together to the evening service. On that evening, the congregation was singing, *He's the Savior of My Soul.* (I had culture shock singing these songs, which to my rock and roll ears seemed like really bad music!) As we approached the punch line, "Jesus, oh my Jesus," I wondered what would happen. I always skipped the lines about Jesus because I just didn't think they were true. But that night I sang, "Jesus, oh my Jesus," with all the sincerity and feeling I possessed. As I did, *I felt as if warm oil was being poured over me from head to toe.* The same thing happened to Anne!

Jesus had poured out His fullness upon us and we had received the beginnings of God's amazing gift! We would never be the same. God was real. He was alive and He heard the prayer I had spoken on the yoga mat earlier that week.

The Living God had actually and tangibly touched *me*. After all the years of trying to reach Him, all the efforts and disciplines, the equation now was wonderfully reversed: God had reached me! Relief and joy washed over my being. That night, we entered into a new life. We had received God's greatest gift! We encountered Jesus.

I was stoked! This was early May 1972. I'm not sure if there ever was an offering taken, but eventually we discharged the $2 obligation! Over the next few months everything in our lives would be restructured. Much later, I connected these significant experiences with these words from John's Gospel:

> *The Word became flesh and made His dwelling among us…full of grace and truth.…From the fullness of his grace we have all received…*(John 1:14,16).

The search for pure water, the dead battery that couldn't get us home, the inability to pay for the repair, and the desire to repay that debt had led us to the waters of life, where we could receive the gift without having to pay! We had received the ancient invitation of God, echoed through the millennia to those who thirst:

> *Come, all you who are thirsty, come to the waters; and you who have no money, come, buy and eat! Come, buy wine and milk without money and without cost.…Listen, listen to Me, and eat what is good, and your soul will delight in the richest of fare* (Isaiah 55:1-2).

We had come to the Waters! We were being washed in a tide of life, saturated with unsullied goodness. Our internal motivation and energies were being transformed. We had found the Source, the Headwaters of everything good and pure.

Grace and the New Creation

What had transpired was far more than we understood.

All Things New

Anne and I were part of the New Creation; the restoration of all things had been released within our inner beings. The grace that brings salvation had now come to us. Really, grace had invaded us and was actively delivering our thinking, feeling, and responses from warped, polluted, and deluded thinking that we had picked up along the way. Our future had overtaken our present. The riches of Heaven stood generously accessible—more than we could comprehend.

All we had to do was *nothing*. All we did was *respond* to this amazing grace. We became hooked on the Presence. We went to meetings whenever we could. No one told us we had to do this. We were hungry and thirsty for the Presence of Jesus. No matter how much we got, we could sense there was more. We pursued a continuous encounter with the Living God—every day!

The Grace of God That Brings Salvation

This mighty change in the way we lived was the result of Grace that appeared to us, finally conquering, as Holy Hubert would say, "our dirty little hearts." (See Titus 2:11-12.) Grace came and rewrote our identities! We welcomed this amazing gift from God. As U2 would later sing:

Grace…takes the blame
…covers the shame
Removes the stain…
(Grace) travels outside…of karma

When she goes to work…You can hear the strings
Grace finds beauty…In everything…[1]

God continually pours His Grace into our world, not to make Himself happy—for He already is—but to share His joy with us!

Grace is the sunny and generous disposition of the Father translated into every aspect of our lives. It is the ability of God Himself to please Himself. It is unearned and undeserved. It flows from His goodness and power, unprovoked by our need or depravity. It is who He is. It fills and liberates us with the uncreated freedom of Heaven. It is a heavenly "Get Out of Jail Free" card! Grace is the necessary practical application of the unlimited love of God toward His darling creature, humankind, who is trapped by the repercussions of relational failure.

Grace changes everything. It carries the potential to deliver us from every manner of corruption inherent in a fallen world. Grace opens up an experiential encounter with God, which emancipates us from corruption! Grace grants permission to *participate in the divine nature!*[2]

Grace is *very* happy! Most scholars consider common Greek to be the original language of the New Testament. In Greek "joy" is *chara*. Grace is *charis*. Our English word *charisma* comes directly from the Greek term meaning "grace gift." Can you see the connection of grace with joy? The more grace I am accessing, the more divine joy pours through my countenance, words, and deeds!

The Sunny Disposition of Grace

This is a good place to pause and consider some words that are descriptive of various temperaments and emotional tendencies. On the left are words that are could describe a person who has a positive emotional state, is pleasant and generally enjoyable to be around. The right column is full of words descriptive of all things dour and unpleasant, the kinds of emotional states we like to avoid. You may want to circle or just mentally check off the words that best describe your condition over the past 72 hours. How much grace is overflowing through you? How do your public and private patterns manifest grace?

Need more grace? No pressure, grace is freely given—many times over!

Overflowing Life	Shriveled Negativity
cheerful	grumpy
happy	crabby
sunny	crotchety
joyous	dour
lighthearted	prickly
bubbly	touchy
exuberant	irritable
radiant	crusty
jubilant	cantankerous
ecstatic	bearish
euphoric	surly
blissful	depressed
kind	petty
elated	petulant
delighted	cross
jovial	critical
friendly	disagreeable
good-humored	stressed out
upbeat	grouchy

Grace and peace to you many times over as you deepen in your experience with God and Jesus, our Master (2 Peter 1:2 MSG).

Let's be clear. God has the brightest, friendliest Personality in the universe. In contrast, institutional Christian religion in general (with glorious exceptions) has often tended toward the negative list.

A Tectonic Shift in Theology

Around the world, the Church is in a dynamic recovery from a shortage of authentic spirituality. There are millions who have become totally addicted to living in the Presence of God! It's not just a worship revolution. A powerful, joyful army is arising from the Holy Place and taking smiles, hugs, and miracles to the streets, bars, and garbage dumps of the world! Grace and peace are multiplying! Many times over.

A tectonic shift is underway from rationally based theology to overflowing life springing from revelation. At present we are both observers and participants in one of the most significant changes in the past five centuries. Across the globe, vibrant movements are flourishing, embracing puzzling signs, miraculous wonders, and ecstatic encounters. Newly minted generations of believers have only known a supernaturally gifted, gracious, and joyful theology of the Holy Spirit working in and through believers. Additionally, thousands upon thousands are migrating from an expression of Christianity limited to rationally based convictions to an expansive true spirituality. They are tapping into active Grace that flows spontaneously from communion with the Uncreated Creator of creation! We are in the midst of a full-orbed reformation of normal Christian life! And these changes are only the beginning. God has more—much more—to unleash into the world!

The glorious, lovely Body of Christ has been restrained from its full potential by a theology largely based in the worldview of the sixteenth-century reformers. These great minds made huge contributions to our views of God, humankind, and all that is. They made history and changed civilization. However, while anchored in the glorious and sovereign majesty of God, reformed theology's *applied* view of our salvation has tended to be *forensic* in its focus. It targets man's crime against God and the subsequent dismissal of charges against the elect.

The great confessions from that era indoctrinate us that humans are by nature sinful and that the moment a person is able to act, he becomes a guilty sinner. For his acts of rebellion—whether great or small, known or unknown, committed or omitted—he reaps separation from God, himself, those around him, and the world in general. As both rebellious and guilty, he fully deserves an eternity of inexpressible pain and horror, far, far removed from any mercy or moderating influence of the Divine Presence. However, there is good news! Fortunately for humans, God is by nature full of mercy and kindness. So rather than giving us what we deserve, He both fulfills and circumvents the justice due His guilty creation and offers His Son as the substitutionary victim of the wrath that is due upon the iniquity of humankind.

All this is true, but is partial Truth! There is more—*much more!* Truth by itself is unbending and razor sharp. Truth alone may not be Truth in love. God's truth is never isolated from His love. Perspective determines experience.

Standing in the plains of eastern Colorado on a clear day, you can see the great ranges of the Rocky Mountains rising to the west. At some points, you may see several hundred miles away to snowy summits in sawtoothed silhouette against the sky. In the morning sun, it is dazzling! What you can't see, hear, or smell is the trout stream bordered by columbine, the elk bugling in the meadow, or the old towns and mines nestled in the canyons. You can't hear the wind in the aspens or the song of a thousand brooks dancing in the rocks. Looking at God in His Totality is even more daunting!

"Good theology" that delineates God's attributes and actions, can fail to bring us into overflowing, abundant life lived *within* Him. When Jesus said, "Abide *in* Me," He was not expressing a rational concept. He was making an invitation to move into the meadows and streams of His own Divine nature and power! And there, in Him, is everything you truly want.

If you abide in Me, and My words abide in you, ask whatever you wish, and it will be done for you. (John 15:7 ESV)

Concentration on the corruption of human nature is a sure way to turn the Good News into bad news. When sinfulness is emphasized, it is experienced. Entire systems of discipleship develop in which failure and defeat is treated as normal. Rather than nurturing spiritual formation, discipleship becomes the art and science of sin management. A slow and uncertain progress in sanctification is all that is expected. "Accountability" becomes the very serious business by which the dogs of depravity are kept at bay by the necessary baring of our regular failures to another.

This is *not* the free gift of overflowing life—life so abundant that it is clearly much more than we can anticipate! God has wiped our slates clear and given us more "gift" than we can ever unpack! He cheerfully and freely has given endless, boundless, extravagant Life with a capital L!

Jesus was not just the solution to the crimes of humankind against God, but the expression of the deepest purposes of the Creator in creating humankind. He demonstrated how humans were meant to live, always beholding the Father, always confident that the Father was pleased! He did on earth what the Father was doing in Heaven. He is the pattern for the New Creation.

Now, in this grace-life, we are declared *more than conquerors* who cannot be separated from extravagant and uncreated love! On Patmos, John had a vision in which he beheld a great, innumerable multitude of redeemed overcomers. He saw recreated humanity drawn from every tribe and tongue and nation, dressed in righteousness and full of splendor. This living sea of humanity is joined in purpose and activity with the heart of God! We are among them![3]

Mystery and Spirituality

Once we start looking, we find the Scriptures are filled with doorways and windows into spiritual encounters that take us beyond reason. Entering into them necessitates leaving logic as our guiding principle and fully leaping into the inscrutable experiences of mystery. This doesn't mean we lose our minds entirely, but we subjugate the mind to the Holy Spirit and what He reveals—even things beyond our understanding.

Jesus regularly said things that could not be rationally digested! "Eat My body and drink My blood" will do for illustration.[4] He didn't worry about explaining things clearly.

Consider, *"The Kingdom of Heaven is like a farmer with a bag of seed..."* (Mark 4:26). That's it? Yes, that's it. It's all that we get, unless we dive in. We can write theology and teach doctrine alluded to in His words, but we can't deny that they are mysterious! They are more caught than taught.

Jesus said that if we've seen Him we've seen the Father! He is the Word of the Father. He is the final explanation!

What does all this mean? That we are drawn beyond the things we can rationally classify and explain into a relationship with the most creative Personality in the universe. This is not philosophy; this is life!

We seek His Kingdom and His righteous nature above all else. He is the wisest of kings and His Kingdom is the realm of *more than* every wholesome human dream and longing! It's *always* much more than. His provisions exceed our wildest imaginations and our deepest needs.

Our relationship to the King and His Kingdom is more romance than reason. It is holistic, fully engaging the spiritual, mental, emotional, and physical faculties. It fills up our senses with sensations of the divine nature. It is active, social, contemplative, and mystical. It is inventive and practical beyond exaggeration. This is "on earth as it is in Heaven" stuff. Jesus said of Himself, "I AM."

Redeemed humans carry the mystery of dual realities within ourselves. Based on what we see in Scripture we're created to fly, to walk on water, to pass through walls, to disappear and reappear. Just maybe not all on the same day. We are created to rule over gravity and solid matter, put the sun on hold, split oceans, stop flooding rivers, cause rivers of water to come out of solid rock, and more. Is it possible that every miracle we see in Scripture is an invitation into Life as it was meant to be?

The Scriptures deliberately provoke us with glimpses of a supernatural life entirely blended with humanness. Jesus, whose single word stilled the storm, was at times weary, hungry, and wondering how long he would be surrounded by a developmentally stunted humanity!

We can easily miss these windows of wonder. It's much easier to concentrate on the important but more mundane moral and ethical issues that are laced through the telling of the amazing God story, the gospel. The ethics are identifiable and subject to classification, debate, and all kinds of scholarly "stuff."

Disturbing social propriety by inviting Himself to dinner at the home of the biggest crook in town, Jesus told the people of Jericho that he came to seek and to save all that was lost (Luke 19:1-10). He doesn't limit this to the lost souls of men, but every aspect of Eden—unhindered perception and intimate relationship with God, each other, and the world around us.

Brilliance is our native condition! We were once dead in trespasses and sins, but now we have been made *alive* together with Christ!

Romance and mystery dance beyond our rational grasp, beckoning us to experience transcendence. This is the call of Grace. Grace is outrageous, beautiful, and mystifying. Grace is eternal. It was in effect before the creation of the universe. Grace flows out of God's joyful, sunny, and generous disposition.

Take a break and consider the brilliance and the romance of God.

He chose us before the world began. The Lamb of God was slain before the world began. It was finished before we began.[5]

It takes my breath away!

We only see through an imperfect lens, peering into the purposes of His unending grace. Even our knowing and prophesying is partial. Yet He has provided for the *full recovery* of humankind, the broken masterpiece of Creation. He invites us into the Reality shared by Father and Son in uncreated bliss!

Full recovery of what? Of everything He intended when He said in Genesis 1, *"Let us make man...."* Can you imagine? Participating in His Divine Nature?

What Is Man?

We might all cry aloud in wonder, "What does it really mean to be human?" We are not just mammals, naked apes who came down from trees, stood upright and began to use fire. We are uniquely endowed with the image and likeness of the Creator of creation. Speaking to *ordinary human beings,* Jesus declared *we* are light in this world! The Scriptures repeat that not only are we the light of the world but that we *are* light! Paul writes, *"You were once darkness, but now you are light in the Lord"* (Eph. 5:8).

We are *now* light! Pure energy. This is not a slight moral improvement. This is a fundamental reconstruction of our nature. It's not in the misty future, but is the present reality of salvation—a new creation. The prophet Isaiah commands God's people to stand up and become light![6] Jesus mandates,

> *Let your light so shine before men, that they may see your good works and glorify your Father in heaven* (Matthew 5:16 NKJV).

See your actions and **glorify** God? Can we even seriously imagine that the Creator of the universe would entrust human beings with improving His reputation? This is almost beyond belief—especially if we take a cursory glance at the state of the Church universal in any given decade. And yet, all of creation is waiting with bated breath, in suspense and excitement, for the sons of God to get their act together and finally reveal who they really are!

This is the future, but it is present now. Not only saints, mystics, and spiritual giants, but ordinary unexceptional believers carry within them such potential that it will result in the deliverance of the physical universe when it is released! How can this be?

The true nature of our new birth holds the key to the true New Age. The Church is the true Human Potential Movement! It's all there in the finished work of the Cross! Jesus is the Door, not just to Heaven, but to the restoration of all things!

Endnotes

1. U2, *Grace*. From http://www.lyrics007.com/U2%20Lyrics/ Grace%20Lyrics.html, accessed December 2009.

2. See Second Peter 1:2-4.

3. See Revelation 7:9 and 19:6.

4. See Matthew 26:26-28.

5. See John 17:24.

6. See Isaiah 60. The prophet Isaiah commands God's people to "Stand up and become light!" That is the most literal translation of the Hebrew text, "qumi 'ori." It is also the exact meaning of the German translation Stehe auf und werde licht!

Mystical Union With God

Such a Great Salvation

Salvation means deliverance, healing, restoration, and everything good. It is so majestic, so resplendent, so breathtaking that it staggers our normal way of viewing and doing life. In Western culture where "getting things done" is a best-selling concept, it is more natural to settle for some practical applications that can be reduced to a daily, weekly, or monthly "to do" list. That is just what religion does.

The salvation God has delivered through the incarnation, the Cross, and the resurrection of Jesus Christ is so huge that without a continual pressing into the full measure of His love, we are in danger of not realizing how Great the Prize! Neglecting to explore our salvation is something like not opening an envelope with $20 billion inside. We are urged by the writer of Hebrews to:

...pay much closer attention to what we have heard, lest we drift away from it. ...How shall we escape if we neglect such a great salvation?... (Hebrews 2:1,3 ESV).

This little passage arrests my attention. There is a danger. The salvation we've been offered is immense. When fully possessed, it will deliver us from all corruption in the universe. This is extreme salvation! Full deliverance into the New Creation will completely vacate all the claims of sin, death, and decay against us. The danger is that we will stop short of full exploration and fail to utilize its rich reserves.

In this failure lies the mediocrity of much contemporary Christianity.

Participation in Divinity

We are invited, even compelled into a great and sumptuous feast the King has prepared for us! It's so extravagant that it defies improvement. It is not a summons to human excellence. No, it's far more! He has richly provided us with everything we need to live supernatural lives. We are invited to actually participate in the Divine Nature and to be totally free from anything rotten or evil![1]

Being forgiven and made new is splendid. Many sincere and godly believers have spent their lives in humble gratitude for this glorious gift. It is beautiful. But there is so much more. We are called to *engage, partake of, and be a participant* in the mystery of His divinity! The very thought of participation in His Divine Nature takes us light years beyond the entry point into the Kingdom of God, deep into the vaulted treasuries of His richest mercies, to the springs of His overflowing fullness of grace!

Jesus said in John 17:3 that eternal life consists of knowing the Father and the Son. To really know the Father and the Son is an unlimited adventure that carries us places that are beyond all we can ask or imagine! The Holy Spirit comes to us as a fountain, a river, a wind, a blazing fire, a faithful herald, and as both Teacher and Guide to the endless beauties and matchless creativity of the Father and the Son.

Filled with fullness and blazing with uncreated energy and love, we are containers of and distribution outlets for the New Creation. This is the true New Age, which will swallow up the old.[2] The regeneration of all things has begun in the heart of every believer who receives the Gift of Life released to us all through the Cross.

Pouring Kindness Into the Infinite Emptiness

The problem is that humankind in general is empty and people are looking in all the wrong places for something to fill them up. Here is a description of the human race:

> *At one time we too were foolish, disobedient, deceived and en-slaved by all kinds of passions and pleasures. We lived in malice and envy, being hated and hating one another* (Titus 3:3).

Despite our best efforts and endless good intentions, most of us find that the life we live fails to correspond to the ideal. The darkness in the human heart is bottomless. Think of Auschwitz. Or 9/11. Darkness twists the hearts.

Outbreaks of unspeakable hatred and cruelty pervade human history. Most of us prefer not to immerse ourselves into the study of the dark side of humankind. Nevertheless, like a thick cloud cover, it dampens our joys and casts a gloom over naive optimism.

Yet into the abyss of human depravity the kindness and love of God pours as an endless Niagara Falls of life. He generously scrubs us clean in ways beyond description. In His saving work, we are immersed in regeneration and renewal. The Holy Spirit thoroughly marinates us in the New Creation, changing our flavor and aroma. The true New Age is unleashed inside us with unrestrained generosity. (See Titus 3:4-7.)

The Holy Spirit delivers the love of God with unstoppable force, like a fire hydrant deep in our hearts. Rivers of living waters flow from deep within our new heart. The Future is continually poured into us. This glory swallows up our personal dim and shameful past!

Jesus said it Himself, *"Behold, I am making all things new!"*[3] This goes beyond making ornery people nice! Properly understood, "rebirth and renewal" is a redefining of all things, past, present, and future! It is real and it's expanding.

For many years, James Daniels, an elderly black gentleman, attended our church. He was a man of few words. No matter what was going on, he would come up and say to me, "Everything's gonna be all right." He believed it, and when he said it, I believed it too. In his last years, he suffered amputations of his lower legs. His words to me never changed. It was true. He lost his legs to diabetes, but he never lost his joy. He was full of light and optimism to his dying day.

And this is the message and the gospel: despite the worst efforts of darkness and human cruelty, everything changed at the Cross! Regeneration and renewal shout from redeemed hearts, "Everything's gonna be all right!"

In fact, the things Jesus has promised are already done! The promised future already exists. We carry this entire dimension of existence within ourselves in His indwelling presence.

The Future Is Now!

On that day you will realize that I am in My Father, and you are in Me, and I am in you (John 14:20).

This is a revolutionary statement. It reverberates with glories that lie beyond the reach of our 3-pound human brains feverishly engaged in logic! Its fullness is outside the realm of reason. These things are made known by revelation and are meant to be experienced.

Revealing the New Reality is the present work of the Holy Spirit, our Guide into all Truth! To fully grasp this takes a lifetime—or more. Yet Jesus said we would know it in *that day.*

What day is "that day?" Is it a distant, future, end-of-all-things time when the entire universe is renovated and all is well, "the sweet by and by"? Or is it *here now,* but still coming? Jesus defines "that day" as a day of knowledge. When that day dawns, we will know, really know by insight and experience the reality of the Son both in the Father and in us. We will *experience* that we are *in* Him. So, is *that day* present or future? The answer is "Yes!" It is both. To the degree that we perceive and enter into experience, "that day" dawns within us!

...You Will Realize That I Am in My Father...

This treasure chest of a verse contains three exquisite gems that sparkle with fire. The *first* is that Jesus is *in* the Father. On the surface, this seems pretty basic. We accept it, that somehow He *exists* within the Father. Truthfully, we don't understand it since it is removed from us by eternity and infinity and all that kind of cosmic stuff. We accept it by faith and are strengthened.

But is there more to this? Does it go beyond theological assent? Is Jesus saying that He *is in* the very *Source of all* things, thus *subject to nothing* else? Is the union so complete, so without reservation or limitation, that the proper way to express it is with words that, if fully embraced, can only leave us dumbstruck in wonder? Yes! Especially if we consider that they were being spoken by a physically diminutive and unimpressive first century Jew who never traveled more than 200 miles from the place of His birth, never owned a house, never wrote a book, never did any of the things that are normally associated with greatness. As a man, He is stating, "*I am* in the Father," not "I will be in the Father"! There is splendor and hidden glory in these words.

...And You Are in Me...

The *second* gem of this "That Day" reality is that we *exist* in Jesus. The ground of our existence has changed. It has returned to the original intent. This is a familiar concept in the writings of the New Testament. Paul's writings are full of this glorious revelation. That we *are* "in Christ" is an enormous matter. If we can totally unpack this in our daily lives, we will be just like Him in just about every way!

This means so much. Paul told the Corinthians that "in Him" they had been made rich in every way! That just about covers everything, doesn't it? Paul said that in Jesus, every promise God has made finds its yes![4] If we are in Him, we are living *in* the uncreated Creator and Ruler of the Universe. It is *impossible* for God to raise us to a higher realm or position than this! This in and of itself is such a great truth that we could spend all of our days exploring and living in its implications and provisions. The glory of these truths cannot be exaggerated! Paul put it this way:

> *Therefore, if anyone is in Christ, he is a new creation; the old has gone, the new has come!* (2 Corinthians 5:17)

We can more or less grasp this. The old has passed away and the new has replaced it. Perhaps more strongly we could put it this way, *"If any man is in Christ, he is (now made of) New Creation."*

Our very being has changed! We are not just *in* the New Creation, New Creation is now what we are! The New Creation is released in us and we become a type of first fruits of all that is to come! *Kingdom Come* has come. The Greek term used for "new" is *kainos*. It connotes new in terms of quality, that which has been previously unknown and is superior to the old as in *"new heaven and new earth."*[5]

...and I Am in You...

The *third* and final gem is that Jesus exists in us. We not only *exist* in Him, but He *exists* in us! Simply, because we live in Him, we are utterly safe and wholly saturated in the continual and wondrous affection of the Father for the Son! He is in the Father and in us all. Jesus simultaneously exists in these two realms of reality—in the Father and in the Church as His Body. Truly He is the Mediator between God and humankind, the man Christ Jesus! There is no separation. God has reconciled all things to Himself in Christ! We cannot be separated from the love of God!

Endnotes

1. See Second Peter 1:3-4.

2. See First John 2:17 ESV.

3. See Revelation 21:5 ESV.

4. See First Corinthians 1:4-5 and Second Corinthians 1:20-21.

5. See Second Peter 3:13.

A Grid for Supernatural Living

There is a progression of unpacking this great salvation we have received. I've discovered some essential sequencing that works itself out in my daily life. It is all rooted in Supernatural Love.

The power of love is released when we stay present in it. He who lives in love, lives in God.

The goal of this section is to raise your awareness of who you are in Him. You are the beloved. You are defined by *agape* love and designed by God to be a super-conqueror.

Where to begin? We begin with Presence—not just His Presence in you, but your presence in Him. All the time. Right now. We will go through it step by step.

Here is the basic grid, with the five areas of focus that can open up the universe to you:

1. I AM   Present in the Moment

2. Radiance   Appreciation—the Light that Shines

3. Integrity   Agape Love—the Ground of All Reality

4. Fullness   The Endless Supply

5. Joy   Entering Into Delight (Jubilee)

CHAPTER 7

Stewards of His Presence

The real place of spiritual power is to be fully present in the Lord and face to face before Him without a trace of shame or the slightest anxiety. The continuous experience of being loved without limit brings unbridled joy and true freedom. Out of that we love both God and our fellow humans as the effect of His love. It takes God to love God.

Without a cloud of judgment or trace of fear for the future, we live in His love, the present powerful joy of the Lord. We hold Him in our innermost being. Infinity, eternity, and perfection have found a home within each of us.

We Bring What He Is

We are the true light bearers. We light up our world. When we walk into a room, all the resources of Heaven come physically into that environment. All the "I AM" statements of Jesus are carried by us into every conversation and interaction. This is the New Creation in overflow.

Take a moment and picture this. When you walk into a room, there is more than meets the eye.

- The *Bread of Life* walks into the room with provision.

- The *Good Shepherd* walks into the room with guidance and protection.

- The *Way,* the *Truth,* and the *Life* is now available to the situation around you.

- The *Resurrection* and the *Life* is there in you to raise the dead!

The implications are mind-boggling.

You carry within you the King and His glory. The power is in our undiminished presence in Him. This is the key to moving into the Power of Presence. Not just His Presence, but my presence and your presence.

The Impossible Command

> **Arise, shine,** *for your light has come, and the glory of the Lord has risen upon you* (Isaiah 60:1).

To me, "Arise and shine" sounds a lot like, "Stand and deliver!" Is this just poetic language, or is God actually calling us into a higher level of living?

To shine is to be a source. Shining is more powerful than reflecting. "Shine" implies that distinct energy can radiate from our presence that can fill emptiness. The words of Isaiah are commands, not suggestions. They are not intended to frustrate, but to open doors of possibility. The literal Hebrew could be translated, "Stand up and be light!" Here is a brief comment from the ESV Study Bible:

> Arise, shine addresses Zion. The bright future of God's people calls for cheerful expectancy now by faith.[1]

Zion is where David erected his Tabernacle. It speaks of a manifested glorious presence of God. It symbolizes an ideal Israel. It is the future.

The New Testament plainly states that we have already come to Mt. Zion.[2]

Zion is not pie in the sky, but is a *fait accompli*. In truth, what is promised to and incumbent upon a millennial Israel is already present in mystery within the redeemed. Your future has already begun. Kingdom Come is here now, as well as continuing to arrive. It's so big that it fills all history. In our current age we live in a tension between the already and the not yet.

Isaiah is not alone in commanding light to shine from God's people.

Shine Like the Sun

Jesus ordered, not suggested:

> Let **your** light so **shine** before men, that they may see your good works and glorify your Father in heaven (Matthew 5:16 NKJV).

He is not commanding generic light to shine but the light we possess. It is *our* light! A surface reading can confine this shining to a kind of ethical superiority. But what if Jesus, like Isaiah, was provoking *the entirely possible* out of the divinely endowed children of the living God? Can this be? Our friend Bill Johnson is very quotable. One of his many aphorisms is, "When the impossible seems logical, you know your mind is renewed."

Speaking of the future, Jesus declared that *"then the righteous shall shine like the sun in the kingdom of their Father…"* (Matt. 13:43).

For us the *then* is present inside the *now* within us. It's still coming, but it is already present. The *already but not yet* was clearly part of the way Jesus saw things.[3] We shine like the sun. It's coming, but it's also here.

How does the sun shine? From a physical point of view, the sun is the source and sustainer of all life on our planet. No wonder the ancients worshiped the sun! Although it is just an average sized star, it is the engine that drives the winds, the hydrological cycle, the ocean currents, and the weather that nourishes life on this planet!

Deep within the core of the sun are gravitational forces so powerful that 700 million tons of primitive hydrogen undergo fusion *every second!* This process yields the conversion of simple hydrogen into 696 million tons of helium per second. What happened to the 4 million missing tons of matter? They are converted into pure energy. Gamma rays that pass through the body of the sun are sufficiently cooled to radiate into space as the energy we know as light. Less than one-millionth of the radiant energy of the sun actually strikes planet Earth. Yet that infinitesimal fraction of the sun's energy gives life, causes hurricanes, and if you get too much of it, can give you a sunburn.

Shine like the sun indeed! Deep within your core are the strong attractive forces of love between the Father and the Son. This is love fusion! It releases enough energy every second to renovate the entire universe. We are participating in this divine love-fest!

Both Isaiah and Jesus are commanding the redeemed to release the creative energies of God—His gracious positivity—into the world around us! We carry the capacity to make our own weather systems, to affect the currents of human culture, to cause the deserts to blossom like the rose, and ultimately to restore all things! We are stewards of the future.

But how can this be? Do we take the statements of Scripture seriously? The full spectrum of our spiritual new nature contradicts virtually all our enculturation and emotional programming. Light is our now reality.

Not Merely Human

John the Beloved, who was transformed by the revelation of supernatural love, saw who we actually are. What he wrote is revolutionary:

> *Beloved, **now** we are children of God; and it has not yet been revealed what we shall be, but we know that when He is revealed, we shall be like Him, for we shall see Him as He is* (1 John 3:2 NKJV).

This is speaking of the present and of progressive development. *"It has not been…"* and *"when He is revealed"* are not restricted to an after-death experience. They also speak of ongoing revelation of who He is and who we are during this lifetime! We are *now* the supernatural offspring of the Creator of all things. It is the luminous effect of being "made alive together" with Christ!

By grace we're forgiven and our résumés of shame are no longer relevant to our future employment! This reality is sovereign, outside of our dim self-evaluations. Yet living in this reality has everything do with our opinions. To fully possess this, we must believe it and live in the victory that overcomes the world. We are no longer merely human! Human reason and effort fail us. We must live by the faith of God!

We are He and He is we. We are so united that we are His Body and He is our Head. We are the beloved offspring of *Melek haOlam,* the King of the Universe who set the stars in their dances.

No wonder Paul reproved the Corinthians for acting merely human—which is quite stunning. People regularly excuse less than perfect behavior with the statement, "After all, we are only human." Not so fast! We are *not* merely human, and if we only act human, we are missing the glorious potential of shining like stars in the midst of a crooked and perverse generation!

> *For you are still carnal. For where there are envy, strife, and divisions among you, are you not carnal and* **behaving like mere men?** (1 Corinthians 3:3 NKJV)

When we were teenagers, my mother would sometimes scold my four brothers and me for acting "like a bunch of pigs!" It was beneath what she expected of us. If we live only like humans, we miss the essence of the new birth!

Divine DNA

Being *like God* isn't a goal we strive to accomplish. The new birth hardwires us to be like Papa! It alters our DNA. We are the offspring of God. The Image and Likeness have been resuscitated. The imperishable seed of the Incarnate Word has taken root. Jesus is the Firstborn of a very large family of siblings! His genetic code is at work and the internal blueprint is guiding every cellular action until together we grow into the stature of the Pattern!

This shining, supernatural life business staggers the natural mind. It is actually quite simple: God is love. Even as infants learn to speak, our new nature learns to love with God's uncreated *agape* love. We become like Him. The good news is that God Himself is our Coach, training us to love one another with championship level abilities and skills. The hardwiring is found in the spiritual DNA we inherit! We need no human instruction in this most fundamental behavior. We are "God-taught" to love each other.

That's the New Commandment that defines the New Creation! Elsewhere we read that even small acts of agape love fulfill the Law, the righteous requirement of God. In other words, loving each other is supernatural living![4] It is the manifestation of the sons of God! A culture of supernatural love is the context for miracles. What we "do" is continually revealing what we "are."

As we will see, there is a practical progression in releasing the Kingdom within. There is a way to unleash the New Creation with useful and delightful results. There is a starting point. There are stages on which to focus your attention as you learn to "be all that you can be." That phrase was used effectively by U.S. Army recruiters for 20 years. Yet it is far more applicable to your potential as a child of God than it ever was for the Army!

Practicing the Power of "Here-Now"

Your energized Life begins with a deliberate presence. When the real you is really present you will shine. That's what light does. It's the light of love, protected by integrity and sustained by continual fullness. All this leads to the ultimate Jubilee—a life of delight, rest, and celebration!

Here is a graphic way to see this.

Presence →
    Light →
        Integrity →
            Wholeness (Fullness) →
                Delight (Joy, Rest, Play)

Power is in Here-Now presence. We are bearing Christ within. You are a container filled with the Age to Come and carrying the Future of All Things! If we really grasp this, we live in holy awe, as stewards and as portals into the heavenly realm. This access is not according to the Law, but according to the glorious grace of God which cannot cease or be destroyed. It is the power of endless, indestructible Life. What He is, we are in the midst of the world!

Endnotes

1. Notes on Isaiah 60:1; English Standard Version (ESV) Study Bible; Copyright © 2008 Crossway Bibles, a publishing ministry of Good News Publishers, Wheaton, IL. All rights reserved.

2. *But you have come to Mount Zion, to the heavenly Jerusalem, the city of the living God* (Heb. 12:22).

3. This mind-set is revealed in Jesus' statement to the woman at the well: *"The hour **is coming**, and **now is**, when the true worshipers will worship the Father in spirit and truth; for the Father is seeking such to worship Him"* (John 4:23 NKJV).

4. For further exploration, read First Thessalonians 4:9-10, Romans 13:10, and Galatians 5:14.

Just Show Up!

Be Here-Now: The Challenge to Be Present

All we have to do is show up…and *stay* present. In our presence, His presence shines. This is precious treasure, great and costly. It is worthy of our conscious awareness, heart, and soul. His presence is **big**. It is not confined to our small human bodies. We've got to let it out.

Filling a Space

I deliberately practice letting His presence out. If you are sitting in a room—perhaps your own home—why not let His manifest presence out? Go ahead, just let your conscious agreement with His presence within you grow. This is a simple exercise of faith.

Do you believe He is present within you? Then let that awareness grow, let the glorious presence of Christ in you become the center of your thoughts and feelings. This is not just an idea. It is wonderful therapy to our emotions. What are His emotions toward you? Does He love you with an everlasting, indestructible affection? Is His grace so great as to render all your failings irrelevant? Did He toss them over His shoulder and forget about them? Is He anticipating your presence at the great wedding supper?

How do you feel when you let His undiminished brilliance wash over your body, soul, and spirit? Now let this joyful feast of unearned love expand beyond your own physical frame and begin to fill the space around you.

Simply by being who you really are in Him, you are fulfilling the command to "arise." You are standing up from spiritual stupor, going higher, and getting clearer. As you go higher, He is being lifted up above all the circumstances, above the music that is playing, above the economy, above politics and all human turmoil. When He is lifted up, He draws all people to Himself.

To increase your presence in His Presence, I recommend that you regularly "let Him out." If you are sitting in a coffee house, or in a park, or on a beach—anywhere where people are gathered—try letting His presence out. Experiment and experience. See if you can radiate and fill a space, charging and shifting the atmosphere to "as in Heaven."

Warning! Very *interesting* things may happen. Love creates the atmosphere for miracles. In Acts 19, it sparked riots. If nothing happens other than becoming more aware of Christ in you, that too is a ***huge*** benefit!

Let's take a break from reading. Relax and focus. You are the Temple. Sink into the core of His heart in you.

You may want to say this. Your words have power:

I am *here* in Him!

I am *now* in Him!

I have no worries, no resentments, no shame! I gave them all away!

I am in bliss (perfect happiness, oblivious to everything else).

This is the place of faith and the place of power. It is so simple, yet so challenging. In the simple awareness of being entirely *here* and entirely *now*, you are wrapped and saturated in Perfect Love. All the resources of Heaven are present within and at your disposal. Your life is hidden with Christ in God! You are experiencing what the Scriptures say about you. It is the place of agreement and the place of power.

What takes us out of the powerful moment? What diminishes the manifestation of His presence?

Enemies of Here-Now

Fear and Worry

Fear and worry rob the connection to the present, the place of faith and power. Fear is an unpleasant emotion that is on alert to danger, pain, and threat. There are times when a fear is healthy.

When I was 16, I was racing downhill on my Yamaha motorcycle. The speedometer read 115 miles per hour. I felt the bike float, losing solid contact with the road. In a flash, I realized that I couldn't take the next turn at that speed. I was afraid to touch the brakes. I backed off the throttle and the bike slowed to 85 before the turn. About a mile later I pulled over, got off, and shook for about ten minutes! I needed a healthy respect for the laws of physics!

Many fears that people experience are not healthy but are the result of replaying past trauma or entertaining imaginary disasters. Full-blown mature love casts false fear out on its ear! Fears and worries take us out of "present Presence" into a false future in which we are on our own, like orphans surviving by our wits. Worries are low-grade fears that separate our emotions from the loving plans of our Father in Heaven.

Disappointment

Disappointments are toxic to our inner being. They make the heart sick, robbing the childlike confidence that we have the best Father in the universe!

Judgment and Unforgiveness

Judgments and the inability to forgive keep us anchored to past trauma. These moments of pain can be like chains that keep us from rising into the absolute freedom and joy of the Father and the Son.

Shame

Shame is a species of unforgiveness toward ourselves. Shame is a painful feeling. It is a sense humiliation and regret triggered by the feeling that "there is something wrong with me." That's the feeling of unrighteousness, often triggered by wrong or foolish behavior. Shame in any of its disguises robs us of our bold joy and shining, confident humility. Shame comes like a cloud over the shining sun and turns the rays of glory inward. It dulls our shine.

Condemnation

Many judgments we have toward ourselves manifest in feelings of depression or condemnation. Condemnation is like a self-effort hospital where we send our soul—our personality—to suffer and be treated until we determine that it is better. This self-judgment is a form of self-reliance, the opposite of the joyful flow of His Presence within us. To all those suffering self-imposed darkness in the "condo-bondo" prison of condemnation, the Holy Spirit pleads as the Counselor of our souls, "Come out! Step out into the glorious sunshine of His love and total, unconditional forgiveness!"

Holiness comes from within! It is His Presence, gloriously burning within that lifts and frees us from all anxiety and all regret. We were created to fly, to soar on the reliable updrafts of joy!

Don't Worry, Be Happy!

This was the title of a hit song by Bobby McFerrin. It won the 1989 Grammy Award for best song. His inspiration came from a famous quote of Meher Baba, the Sufi mystic popular in the 1960s. But long before Baba or McFerrin, Jesus had declared this maxim of abundant life.

Many see the Sermon on the Mount as the opening address of the ministry of Jesus. It is the announcement that Heaven is on the offensive, invading the dark negative lives of people and nations, taking back what Adam lost. This will continue until all things are restored to their pristine state—or better! He came to make all things new.

During this opening salvo on the fallen state of humanity He commanded us to not worry not once but three times! What did He actually say? Here are some brief excerpts:

> *I tell you,* **do not worry** *about your life...*

> *So* **do not worry,** *saying, "What shall we eat?" or "What shall we drink?" or "What shall we wear?" ...your heavenly Father knows that you need them. But seek first His kingdom and His righteousness, and all these things will be given to you as well.*

> *Therefore* **do not worry** *about tomorrow, for tomorrow will worry about itself. Each day has enough trouble of its own* (Matthew 6:25,31-34).

Three times! Do not worry! These are prescriptions for freedom and joy.

Worry is a rampant plague among the human race. Of all creatures, only humans worry. We tend to worry about finances, relationships, world events, the price of almost everything. It's as if the entire weight of the world rests upon us. Though worry robs and kills us, we allow it as normal.

Worry shouts deep within our beings that we are orphans—street children who have to survive—always on guard against threats and shortage. Worry is nothing but a low-grade, chronic expression of fear. There is nothing pleasurable in worry; it distracts us and interrupts our participation in God's goodness. Worry blinds us to our heavenly Father's care for us today, tomorrow, and always.

Cured of Worry

So what's the cure? Seeking His Kingdom. In it we find assurance, provision, and release. Eugene Peterson's *The Message* paraphrases this passage:

> *What I'm trying to do here is to get you to relax, to not be so preoccupied with getting, so you can respond to God's giving.... Steep your life in God-reality, God-initiative, God-provisions. Don't worry about missing out. You'll find all your everyday human concerns will be met.*
>
> *Give your entire attention to what God is doing right now, and don't get worked up about what may or may not happen tomorrow. God will help you deal with whatever hard things come up when the time comes* (Matthew 6:31,33-34).

Relax...God has it all covered. Become as a child. Often the most childlike are the most trusting.

Rather than worry, we are invited to live in continual joy—blissed out and only aware of the Father's love. Worry is the enemy of the Powerful Present in which faith lives and moves. It pulls us into a distorted house of mirrors of a nonexistent future without the love of the Father that is present in our lives.

Worry is toxic to abundant life. Don't worry—we are commanded to live in continual joy! My oldest grandson is only nine, but he still can get stressed out. We were standing in line for the wildest ride at an amusement park. It was his "bragging rights" ride so he could tell all his friends. *The Mind Eraser* hits 92 mph. It's sheer terror or joy, depending on your disposition. I was the oldest person in line by at least a decade. He was one of the youngest. So I asked if he was worried. He told me that he often hears a voice inside him saying:

> *Rejoice in the Lord always. Again I will say, rejoice!*

That's a good thing to hear.[1]

We are invited to a continual feast! Happiness is our place at the table set before us by the Lord our Shepherd! It is the drink from the overflowing cup of His goodness and mercy.

So, one more time, in case we forget: *Don't worry. Be happy! Be Here-Now!*

Simplicity and the Miracle Tire

Present in the moment, with childlike faith, great miracles seem normal. Sometimes we know too much to have simple faith. Our sophistication can get in the way.

During the spring and summer months of 1972, Anne and I were drawn to Jesus. We were experiencing a steep learning curve regarding the ways of God. Week by week, our worldview was being rewritten, not only by doctrine, but by the miracles that occurred around us.

We had gathered in the living room with about 70 other young people to worship God and to share fresh insights and experiences. Just as we were getting started, three friends came bursting through the door. Their faces were aglow with holy awe as they told what had just transpired.

Rocky, Keith, and Heidi had driven an old pickup truck down into a steep river canyon, over miles of dirt road, until they came to a place on the river where there was a pool, a beach, and sparkling sunlight. They parked their truck and climbed down a small cliff with their guitars to the beach below. Accomplished musicians, they spent the afternoon there and wrote several new songs the Lord gave them.

Naked Hippie Invasion

Later in the afternoon a group of about 30 hippies arrived by a dirt road on the other side of the river. As this group found a beach area across from my friends, they began taking off their clothes and went "skinny dipping" in the clear waters of the Stanislaus River. Rocky and Keith felt like they should leave. As they were climbing up the cliff, Heidi stopped and told the guys that she thought they were making a mistake. She saw this as an opportunity to worship and share the good news of Jesus. So they returned to the beach and began to play their guitars and sing some of the beautiful songs they had written.

Soon a number of the naked hippies swam over to them and were drawn by not only the music, but by the tangible presence of God. Our friends shared the message of Jesus and a number of the young hippies believed in Jesus. The afternoon passed quickly in true joy and love. When it was time to leave, two of these new converts asked if they could get a ride back into town. A young man and a teenage mom with her nursing baby joined the climb back up the cliff to the waiting '53 Chevy pickup.

No Spare

Much to my friends' disappointment, the right front tire was completely flat. They had no spare. Heidi sat in the cab of the truck, resigned that this was going to be a very long day. On the outside, Rocky and Keith were discussing the best course of action. One of them would have to roll the wheel out to the highway, miles away and mostly uphill. Then catching a ride to a service station would be the next challenge. How much money did they have? Would it be enough?

As they were considering these dismal prospects, the young man who had just met Jesus an hour or two earlier asked, "Why don't you pray and ask God to fill the tire with air?" So they did!

Sitting in the cab with her head down on the dashboard, Heidi felt the right side of the truck lift. She assumed the guys were jacking up the truck to take off the wheel. She was confused when Rocky jumped in behind the steering wheel with a huge smile and started the engine, put in the clutch, and shifted into gear.

Heidi asked, "What are you doing?"

Rocky and Keith rejoiced together, "God just healed the tire! Hallelujah!"

Touching the Miracle!

A wave of astonishment washed over them. They trusted God and found themselves riding back to town on a miracle! Brimming with joy, they pulled up to the meeting, which had already begun. Faces aglow, they threw open the door and blurted out the story!

At that, all of us jumped up and ran out of the house and across the street. Many of us touched the dusty, bald tire that God had miraculously filled with air. It was Here-Now!

I had no logical explanation. It was simply astounding. Wonder brings us into the present. I knew deep within that no one could make this up! Their faces beamed with God-light. Their Father in Heaven knew their need! They needed to get to the meeting. I needed to believe without doubt that God was personal, real, and active. No brilliant debater or atheist could ever take that experience from me! No one could ever convince me or the other 69 people that night that the tire was anything less than a small miracle!

After nearly 40 years, the story still thrills me! Do I know why God filled a tire with air that time and might not another time? Absolutely not. As our friend Heidi Baker says, "He's God and I'm not. Hooray!" Is He capricious? Never. He's a good Dad. We have the best Dad in the whole world!

Perhaps God's actions toward these young believers finds a bit of analogy in the spontaneous joy of parenting young children. When our children were small, we would occasionally surprise them with something wonderful—like a trip to Disneyland. If the surprise was just at the right time, the kids would jump and shout with delight. But most days, they did their chores and homework.

The tire was a lesson in God's surprising grace. It taught me and still teaches me, "Don't worry! Be happy!"

Be Here-Now.

Endnote

1. This encouragement is found in Philippians 4:4 (here quoted from the NKJV).

Shared Reality

Sorting through more than 500 years of theology is daunting. There is so much to say about God, about man, about sin and salvation and angels and everything else important. Entire libraries are filled with the deep insights of godly scholars and mystics who've gone before. Among these writings are the riches passed on by true spiritual fathers and mothers. We gratefully stand on their shoulders and see things that were hidden in their day.

Each generation must carry on the challenge of pioneering new territory. God's story is not complete. We are part of the age-long treasure hunt. Although the canon of Scripture has been completed and mostly agreed upon, rich and untapped veins of glory remain to be mined!

All faith involves risk *and* reward! Thank God for spiritual pioneers. Pioneers press into territory that is not safe. Pioneers have a higher mortality rate than the settlers who come after. After pioneers survive and thrive, the settlers move in.

Around the world today millions of believers are prepared to "risk it all" and go where no one else wants to go. They are energized by "present truth," the fresh insights of the past 15 years. Things go back much further, of course, and many current "present truths" were first uncovered by others. The Church, after all, is God's long-lived, colorful family and the family tree is full of interesting and sometimes zany characters.

The River of God

For at least the past 15 years, there has been a glorious emphasis on the Father's affection for His children. Millions upon millions have been affected by the outpouring of the Holy Spirit that touched down, among other places, in Toronto in early 1994. Spreading like water, the love, spontaneity, and supernatural power that was welcomed by this move has translated into an unprecedented wave of missionary expansion.

We always were seeking revival and pressing in for more of Jesus. That's just how we live. In September 1994, Anne and I made a brief and seemingly uneventful visit to what is now the Toronto Airport Christian Fellowship. We weren't sure what to do with our experiences and observations there. We decided to do nothing.

The Holy Spirit surprised us the following Sunday morning in our regular service. I gave an ordinary altar call, but there was an extraordinary response. An unusually large number of people came forward, stretching from wall to wall at the front of the auditorium. Anne joined me to pray for the people, which was also unusual at that time. With simple prayers like, "More, Lord," the people began to shake, weep, jump, laugh, and/or fall down! More people came. It went on for a few hours in an unexpected flood of power, joy, and holiness. This outpouring of glory continued. For at least four years, our normal services were radically altered. Week after week, we were blasted by powerful waves of God's Presence. These onslaughts of Heaven changed the way we came together. Sometimes so many people were shaking, crying, laughing, and falling that it was impossible to conduct a reasonable order of service. On several occasions, our entire worship team fell down—microphones and all.

To some, this move seemed bizarre and disorderly. They left and went to more conventional churches. For us, it felt like we had returned to our Jesus Movement roots. Miracles occurred spontaneously. Incurable diseases were cured without any special prayer. People got used to being smashed, mushed, shaken, burned, and overwhelmed by the Holy Spirit. Some were destabilized. Many more were healed. Lukewarm believers were filled with a new love for God's Presence and His Word. Marriages were restored. "Renewal babies" were conceived. Love was in the air. Night after night, meetings would go on until 2:00 or 3:00 A.M.

At that time we were in a very rough part of town, meeting in what had once been a casket factory. Previously we had to hire off-duty policemen on Sunday mornings to deter disruptions and thefts, however during the season of these meetings, there were no late-night incidents.

I would sometimes stand up during the wildest and silliest meetings and declare, "This is not *it*. But, it's getting us ready for *it,* and if we will continue to pursue His Presence, we will be sending our ministers, ministries, and missionaries beyond our wildest dreams!"

I wondered why I would say these things. They would just come out of my mouth. Now, 15 years later, I look back and see it was all true. We are sending out more missionaries than I ever dreamed. They go to the poorest people and the poorest nations. The go to state houses and legislatures. They work on global strategies and they simply stop to love the one. They share the glories of the Lord in churches and in bars.

We are just one expression of this next wave of glory that is coming from Heaven. There are millions and millions of believers on every continent who are living out of a fresh paradigm based on God's loving Presence acting through them. Through the River of God's presence, the Great Commandment has become the foundation for the Great Commission!

Through the continual saturation of God's Presence, the Church has changed its view of itself. Today it is normative for young believers to believe that they are supernaturally birthed and gifted. They are the army and the solution God has deployed into the darkness. They are not mere

men and women. They are the offspring of God, predisposed by the ge-
netics of the New Birth for victory over the broken world system![1]

A Shared Life With God

What is the essence of this victorious living? It is the joyous, uninterrupted, unclouded reality of a shared life with God Himself! It is
complete joy all the way around. This is the way it was in Eden. This is
the way it was before Eden, before creation.

That which was from the beginning was the shared reality enjoyed
by the Father and the Son. God entered into our world to apply His joy
as the cure for human sadness. God the Son became the Son of Man
so that the sons and daughters of men might be restored to full access
to the reality of true fellowship between the Father and the Son. There
is *no separation!*

> *We proclaim to you what we have seen and heard,* **so that** *you
> also may have* **fellowship** *with us. And our* **fellowship** *is with
> the Father and with His Son, Jesus Christ. We write this to
> make our* **joy complete** (1 John 1:3-4).

This is all about increasing joy! The beloved John and company saw
it, heard it, and touched it. They declared it so that we can enter into
the same reality. This is the true meaning of *fellowship*. The Greek term
translated *fellowship* is *koinonia*. As used in the New Testament it meant
a common life or a shared reality. John wants us to *share his reality!* The
reality he is living is the reality shared by the Father and the Son!

Selah!

This is huge.

Pause.

Let it sink in.

So What's This Thing Called "Fellowship"?

As new believers, Anne and I were taking it all in. Having no background in American religion, we were looking for every opportunity to

get into the Kingdom of Heaven more deeply than we had before. One Sunday, a young friend approached us after church and invited us to come over to his family's home for *fellowship*. He told us that Steve and some of the other leaders, our new role models, would be there.

We had never heard the word *fellowship* used this way before. I knew some post-graduate students who had fellowships with a university, which gave them stipends to tide them over while pursuing their advanced studies. But this was obviously different.

So, at the appointed time, we drove over in our purple VW bus, not knowing what to expect. What we found was our friends hanging out, watching a San Francisco Giants baseball game on television, drinking Cokes, and grilling some hamburgers and hot dogs! That was not what I had imagined. Anne and I were still just fresh out of Eastern religions and concern about diet was still a big part of our thinking. We were vegetarians and were very careful to eat nonprocessed, organic vegetarian food.

We didn't eat meat—especially not hot dogs! We didn't drink Cokes and we didn't eat potato chips. Not wanting to be rude, I asked meekly if they had any oranges. Fortunately they did. Later on our spiritual journey, we noticed that some churches had a "Fellowship Hall" where people would have donuts and coffee or potluck meals or other functions. All this can be good stuff, but donuts and coffee are *not necessarily* what *fellowship* means in the New Testament!

There is more! We are invited to join into the unimpeded bliss that crashes in great waves of delight between the Father and the Son. The Father sees matchless perfection and glory in the Son, and with the entire honor He can give, He declares the immeasurable worthiness and beauty of the Son. The Son receives this love from the Father. Now the Son beholds the Source of All That Is, and can only return tsunamis of limitless affection, articulate love, and glory to the Father. We are invited into this reality of uncreated love and unending life! John's joy is complete! He has so fully entered into the fellowship of the Father and the Son that he shares their feelings, their desire that all creation would come and enter into the pleasures of God! *This is fellowship!*

Is It Spiritual to Eat Meat?

A month or two after the "fellowship" experience, we were seriously questioning whether it was spiritually good for us to eat meat. Most of the people around us were all American omnivores. God was freeing us from our "enlightenment by diet" mind-set.

Our prayer was simple, "God, if it's good for us to eat meat, please show us."

Twenty minutes later, the phone rang. It was our friend Tim. Tim and Steve were both single and both young, dynamic ministers, who seemed to really know God and live in special communion with Him. They had rented a house on a ranch. They thought that it would be a real blessing to supply their friends and needy people with fresh eggs. So they had bought 100 pullets from a feed store about a month earlier.

On the phone, Tim asked me, "Do you remember the 100 little chicks we bought? It turns out that 12 of them are roosters."

"Oh," I replied, wondering why he called.

Tim continued, "We were praying about what to do with them and felt the Lord told us to give them to you and Annie."

Wow! In only 20 minutes, God had answered our prayer and rearranged our lifestyle!

I told Tim that was great. He told us he would see us that evening at a meeting and bring the roosters.

I got off the phone and couldn't wait to tell Anne about this amazing answer to prayer! Not only did God answer our question regarding the eating meat, He even was sending us some chicken!

We went to the meeting and in my mind I expected to bring home some packages of chicken meat. After the meeting, Tim took us to his car and opened the trunk. In the trunk were three big gunny sacks with the necks tied. Inside each sack were four young roosters that were very much alive! Oh my! Welcome to the food chain!

The next day, we went over to my parents' house to process our answered prayer. Behind the house, the yard sloped uphill with a stump at the top, which served as a chopping block.

Using a double-bladed axe, I proceeded to dispatch the first cockerel. Unfortunately I cut the head off above the vocal cord. Once the axe struck, the "chicken with its head cut off" thrashed about in jerks and spasms. With each convulsion, the beheaded bird made a horrendous squawk. With each squawk, a great fountain of blood spurted out! It was total chaos! The headless fowl bounced, rolled, and jerked its way downhill toward where Anne and my parents' dachshund, Thumper, were standing against the back wall of the house. Anne cowered. Thumper barked and snarled like crazy, but as the blood-spewing creature got closer, he turned tail and ran, yelping in fear!

After that first disaster, I devised a better system and made sure the axe fell below the vocal chords. Soon we had 12 headless roosters. We dipped them all in a big pot of boiling hot water, which allowed us to pluck the feathers, They came out in wet, smelly globs. After singeing off the pin feathers, we dressed the carcasses and packaged them for freezing.

A few days later, we invited Steve and Tim over for some good fellowship and some rooster cacciatore. Getting out our best and biggest cast iron skillet, we simmered the sauce and the fowl for hours on our little woodstove. We were so proud to serve this meal; confident it was spiritually permissible to eat meat. Unfortunately for us, about half of these little roosters must have been lifting weights, because they were so tough! So we chewed and chewed and laughed about the rubber rooster that we served that night.

Participation in the Divine

Fellowship is a big deal. We share life and reality with each other. We eat together, love, and laugh. We weep together and share tragedies as well as triumphs. But true fellowship is beyond human bonding. We are invited into fellowship with the Father and the Son. He makes His reality to be our Reality. We actually get to *participate* in the Divine Nature that flows back and forth on great waves of joy as the Holy Spirit moves between Father and Son! Peter gives us hints of this in these words:

> ...***you may participate in the divine nature*** *and escape the corruption in the world caused by evil desires* (2 Peter 1:4).

We live like Him. We share His nature. We are granted permission to *participate* in the Divine Nature, the "Godness" of God! What makes God to be God is now accessible to us. Some translations translate *participate* as "partake." Either way it is *Mm-mm good!*

This is through the amazing provision of his **great** and **precious** promises! It is His oath, His covenant toward us that opens up this possibility. When we dive right into the pleasures of the Divine Nature we find escape from the futility and death that is in the world through unbridled and corrupt desires.

If you pause and really let this sink in, you may want to shout with all the saints and angels, "Hallelujah, for the Lord our God, the Almighty reigns!" What a Kingdom and what a King!

This fellowship, this participation in the pleasures of God is the reward of being Here-Now. My presence becomes aglow with the uncreated energies of holy love. I begin to overflow with rivers of life-giving water. I become a manifestation of His goodness shining in the midst of darkness.

All this flows through the continual experience of God's love for us. Move in and put down roots in the land of love. It makes you like Him!

> *And so we know and rely on the love God has for us. God is love. Whoever lives in love lives in God, and God in him. In this way, love is made complete among us so that we will have confidence on the day of judgment, because **in this world we are like Him*** (1 John 4:16-17).

We are like Him! He shines and we shine! He is the Bread of Life and we bring nourishment from Heaven to the hungry. He is the Good Shepherd and we bring the present reality of His wisdom, guidance, protection, and provision into every situation. Can you see this? When we are centered and truly present in Him, He is available as the Door, the Gateway into infinite life and possibilities. Just our presence brings "the Lord is my Shepherd" and all of Psalm 23 into the atmosphere of any room! The Beginning and the End of all things is here, manifesting eternal purpose, opposing the emptiness and nihilism of humanism. We bring the overflowing joy and playfulness of the Creator's Wisdom who found delight in the children of men!

CHAPTER 10

Glow in the Dark

In November 1972, Anne and I were on a mission. We wanted to bear fruit. Free and complete salvation by the generosity and kindness of God hadn't really sunk in. Grace and joy had not totally connected. We were getting serious in our efforts to please God. Although we had been handed the greatest gift in the universe, we just didn't fully comprehend it. We wanted to have fruit so that we could be sure we were really saved. And to us, at that time, "fruit" meant leading people to Jesus.

Fishing for Souls

So there we were, driving around in our purple bus, looking for hitchhikers and others who might seem likely to be receptive to the Good News of Jesus. We drove up the mountain on California

Highway 108. An early snow was falling, which added to the fun. About five miles from our house we spotted a young man with waist-length hair. Both his hair and the blue, down parka he wore were totally soaked from the heavy wet snowfall. On top of that, he was standing on the wrong side of the highway, facing in the wrong direction, and hitchhiking with apparently no expectation of being picked up.

He seemed like the perfect candidate! So I swung into a parking lot and turned around, crossed the highway, and stopping near him, asked with a big grin, "Would you like a ride?"

"Uh, sure," was his muttered reply. I then noticed he was carrying an enormous book, about the size of a small suitcase, complete with handles. He got in the back of the van. I asked where he was going to which he replied, "Nowhere really."

His name was Mark. We took him home to our little 9 foot by 21 foot caretaker's cottage. I built a fire in the woodstove, and Anne prepared some hot cocoa. When he warmed up enough to take off his parka, we discovered that he wasn't wearing a shirt.

Urantia Is Alien for Earth

The book he was carrying was *The Urantia Book*.[1] I had heard of it when I lived in Berkeley. It is a book of esoteric teachings about Jesus and other philosophical views. Urantia devotees believe that the book was authored by 23 extraterrestrials that were brought to earth in a flying saucer to spiritually guide the human race. According to its views, Jesus was an alien. In its 2,000 pages was a message for earthlings who lived on *Urantia*, the alien name for Earth. I had a vague awareness of it because I had regularly walked by a restaurant on a corner of Telegraph Avenue and Haste Street in Berkeley that had the Urantia story colorfully painted on its exterior as a huge two story mural—flying saucers and all!

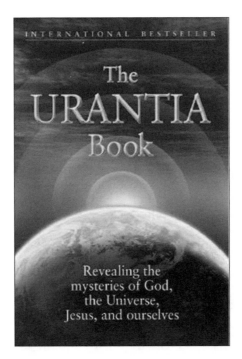

The method Mark used to find spiritual guidance was to set the book on its spine and let it fall open. He believed that whatever fell before the eyes was the message of God to him. That day, every passage had to do with death. He had lost all hope of living and resigned himself to die on that very day, which is why he was standing in the wet snow, getting colder and wetter by the minute. He didn't really expect to get picked up, but sort of imagined he would wander into the woods, sit down, and die of hypothermia. Instead, we picked him up!

Over the cocoa, we shared our own testimony of finding Jesus with Mark. He eventually told us he had been living in a house about a mile away with two hippies, Bowen and Barbara, who were acquaintances of ours. Once he was dry and warm, we took him back to their house.

"Om" for Supper

Bowen and Barbara asked us to stay for dinner. We sat down to a meal of brown rice, sprouts, and wild mushrooms. As Bowen and

Barbara chanted "Om" before the meal, we quietly but forcefully spoke in tongues. We had been delivered from "Om" and didn't want it back! Picking up chopsticks, we enjoyed the food and visiting with our hosts.

All during the meal, Mark stood in a corner of the room facing the wall and said nothing. Bowen told us that Mark had taken a lot of LSD and other psychedelics, pretty much frying his brain. At times he would be violently overtaken with despair and throw himself into the fire in the huge fireplace at the Lodge at Bear Valley, a ski resort about 50 miles away. This sounded like a story straight out of the Gospels—demons and all.

To my disappointment, the conversation didn't really go anywhere that opened up for sharing Jesus. As the meal ended, we thanked our hosts and prepared to leave. I was feeling a little frustrated that there seemed to be no openness to Jesus. (I hadn't learned all this stuff about bringing the Presence of Heaven into any situation.)

You Have the Truth

But as we stood up, Mark wheeled around and said in a very loud voice, "Wait! Don't go!"

I asked him why we shouldn't leave.

He answered, "Because you have the Truth."

We were all amazed at this sudden outburst. This was the open door we had been looking for! Mark and I left the large kitchen and sat down in the living room in front of a fire in the fireplace.

He was completely receptive. I shared with him the things I knew. I told him that Jesus is the Way, the Truth, and the Life. Buddha wasn't the Way. Krishna wasn't the Way. Mohammed is in his grave, but the grave of Jesus is empty. Nietzsche is dead, but God is alive. The Bible was given through inspiration, not delivered from a flying saucer.

A thick and tangible presence of the love of God filled the room. Many rich truths beyond my understanding flowed through me like a prophetic river. I had never heard the terms before, but I prayed that he would be "baptized with the love of God." We prayed for Jesus to totally deliver him of bondage and oppression. He confessed that he believed Jesus was Lord and surrendered his life. Mark became a new creation. His eyes filled with peace. His words become words of hope.

We left and connected with Mark again the next day. He moved into a communal discipleship house called *The Order of the Lamb*. After about a week, he left the house and moved back to his parents' home in the Bay Area. I then lost track of him.

A Shining Face

About two years later, Anne and I were skiing in Bear Valley. As we were getting off the chairlift at the top of Mt. Reba, someone shouted, "Hey Charley!"

I looked and saw a small man with long hair and wire rimmed glasses. He was wearing a brightly colored South American balaclava. It was Bowen. I hadn't seen him since that night at his house with Mark.

"You're the one who saved my friend, Mark!" He shouted at the top of his lungs.

Feeling a little self-conscious in the crowd of skiers gathered at the top of the mountain, I replied in a loud voice, "It was Jesus who saved him."

But Bowen would not be persuaded, "You saved my friend!" he shouted again.

Then he told me that Mark had been completely delivered of his crazy ways. He never again tried to throw himself into a fire or wander aimlessly in the freezing cold. Since that encounter with Jesus in the living room, he was in his right mind and had become a successful representative for Celestial Seasonings tea company. The total change for Mark began that night in Bowen's living room.

Bowen then told me that he poked his head in to see what this "Truth" was that Mark had declared I possessed. As he heard me talking about Jesus as *the Way* to the Father, it offended him to the point that he was going to ask me to leave.

But as he began to enter the room and speak he was stopped in his tracks by a supernatural phenomenon. *My face was shining with light!* Bowen was Jewish and knew the story of Moses coming off the mountain of God with a shining face. Based on that, he decided he wouldn't mess with something that might be God at work.

That was the first time I had heard the story. My face had shone in the dark! It was a good thing I didn't know right away, or I might have had a bunch of T-shirts made and started "Glowing Face Ministries!"

In the past few years, I've had a few people come to me after meetings and tell me that while I was speaking, they saw that I was surrounded by light. As far as I know, it is a bit random. I'm not aware when it is occurring. But I'm always really glad to hear these reports of supernatural light peeking out. The Light is in every child of God.

Glowing and God's Love Light

Here-Now presence is the "set up" for shining participation in the Divine Nature! Here-Now and continually present in His love, with no worries frightening us and projecting a false future, with no shame or resentment anchoring us to the traumas of the past, we are fully alive in Him. His Nature, Uncreated Love, radiates from the core of our being! God has decided to forget every wrong thing we have ever done and replace our own consciousness with His own!

His personality is grafted into us at the level of thought and intention. We shine with this glory. He lights our inner fires, and we blaze with His holy passions!

As a young Christian, I heard the term "on fire" used to describe those who were particularly zealous and energized in their lives. The love of Jesus was like a blazing light within them.

Stars and Auras

Every human being radiates a unique core essence. Some see it as an "aura" or feel it as "vibes." Early depictions of saints typically portrayed their heads surrounded by an orb or halo of light.

Through the centuries, there have been reports of the phenomenon of light-emitting believers. Rays of light shone from the face of Moses after his encounter with God on Mt. Sinai. This perception of power caused the Israelites to hold him in awe. My friend Bowen's reaction was entirely biblical!

The rays of light coming from the face of Moses were connected in concept to the horns on the altar in the tabernacle. Some scholars believe that the "radiance of God's power beaming from Moses' face was fittingly described as horn-like.[2] Subsequently, horns were put on the altars to focus the symbolic presence and power of God."[3]

In the account of Jesus' mountaintop transfiguration, His face shone like the sun. Even His clothes flashed like lightning, so bright was the white!

There are numerous records of monks and other saints throughout history who would "light up" when particularly filled with the Holy Spirit.

> Princess Elizabeth of Hungary (1207-1231) would have roses miraculously appear in her apron as she went about bringing food to the poor. Her spiritual director, Father Conrad, told of her raptures of love, "and how her countenance would seem to give forth rays of light after her secret prayers."[4]

Many more, including Teresa of Avila and Ignatius of Loyola have glowed and brightened rooms during their times of intimate communion with God.[5]

Sometimes the energy is subtle. We colloquially express our perception of this radiance as "vibes." The truth is that we frequently sense something emanating from a person. We call it many things, but every human has a unique electromagnetic field and a unique wavelength. Some transmit more powerfully than others.

Dangers of Radiant Darkness

Not all radiance is good. It can be lustful, greedy, fearful, or hateful. This dark energy is very dangerous. It is based in an insatiable emptiness. Like a vampire, it lives from the life of its victims. Jesus said:

> *...If...the light* [energy] *that is in you is darkness, how great is that darkness!* (Matthew 6:23 NKJV)

Many people radiate something other than the pure love of God. We can be filled with darkness and actually radiate this as light, which is actually a kind of anti-light. This is the realm of deception. This is the effect of powerful, unholy desire.

We don't shine on our own! We are like human light bulbs—we must be connected to a power source! That source can be positive or negative. The *connection* comes through *vision*, the focus of the "eyes" of the heart. Humans are a bit like capacitors in an electronic circuit. We absorb a charge of energy, store it up, and release it.

We were originally created to carry the totally positive energy of God's love. God *is* love. God *is* light. In Him is no darkness at all. There is nothing negative or lacking in God. If the eye of our heart is continually focused on the ultimate positivity of God, then that pure radiant energy will fill our body (the physical vessel in which the essence of our life is carried).

Jesus was very clear, *"The eye is the lamp of the body"* (Matt. 6:22 ESV). This is not speaking of the physical eye, but of a spiritual eye. Paul the apostle prayed specifically that light would shine on the eyes of our heart.[6] We are energized by the focus of our hearts. If we are focusing on those things that are bright and beautiful, then that is what fills us with energy. Here again, *The Message* gets my attention:

> *Your eyes are windows into your body. If you open your eyes wide in wonder and belief, your body fills up with light. If you live squinty-eyed in greed and distrust, your body is a dank cellar. If you pull the blinds on your windows, what a dark life you will have!* (Matthew 6:22-23 MSG)

Negativity comes in many varieties. It damages and destroys our true identity. It is a disease of the soul! It robs not only our personal potential, but it robs the world around us of the creative, loving light that we are intended to release into the world.

Some people are so full of a negative kind of energy that it palpably *radiates*. A man or a woman can powerfully radiate sexual desire. It is a very tangible energy. Some are filled with pride, arrogance, lust, or greed. Although it is darkness, based in emptiness and craving, there is an undeniable energy to it. There are unseen personalities at work.

These dark energies can seem beautiful, powerful, sensual, or they can take on many other guises. A person can be energized and driven by a vision of great wealth. If there is no God-given purpose to the wealth beyond selfish desire, the "light" is darkness. The attractions are really like lures for fish—spiritual black holes that suck victims into oblivion.

In Chapter 2 I mentioned Dr. Timothy Leary, the famous Harvard psychology professor who started the Harvard Psilocybin Project in the fall of 1960 along with Dr. Richard Alpert. After leaving Harvard in 1963, he became one of the father figures of the burgeoning psychedelic drug culture. At the *Human Be-In* in Golden Gate Park, in early 1967, he told the assembled thousands that they needed to "turn on, tune in, and drop out."

In 1969, as a student in Berkeley, I was invited into a small meeting with Timothy Leary. I wanted to meet this man who had made such an impact on the culture of my generation. When I walked into the room,

I felt such a strong sensual power about Dr. Leary that I sensed—even as a pre-Christian—there was something predatory about the energy coming from him.

This helped to spare me from going down a very dark road. Someone must have been praying for me!

Choose Light

There are so many possibilities. When we choose light the result will be that our entire lives will continually fill and refill with a radiance of love, wisdom, and generosity. Good vision produces life, health, and well being in our personalities or souls. Out of that inner vibrancy comes a propensity for success in every undertaking. And we want to pass it forward!

I echo the sentiments of the apostle John as he writes his friend:

> *Beloved, I pray that in all respects you may prosper and be in good health, just as your soul prospers* (3 John 2 NASB).

I like the phrase *"in all respects"!* That just about covers everything. The root of success lies in our personalities being filled with light! I pray that your soul would overflow with light and that health and success would emanate from the love of God within.

Endnotes

1. Urantia Foundation, *The Urantia Book* (Chicago: Urantia Foundation, 1955).

2. "…he did not know that the skin of his face shone and *sent forth beams* by reason of his speaking with the Lord" (Exodus 34:29 AMP).

3. R. Laird Harris, editor, *Theological Wordbook of the Old Testament* (Chicago: The Moody Bible Institute, 1980), Article 2072 Hebrew: qeren.

4. The radiance of God's power beaming from Moses' face was fittingly described as horn-like (Exodus 34:29; cf. also Habakkuk 3:4). Subsequently, horns were put on the altars to focus the symbolic presence and power of God. It was especially on these horns that blood to atone for original and unwitting sin was to be applied (Exodus 30:10; Leviticus 4:7 et al.).

5. John Crowder, *The Ecstasy of Loving God* (Shippensburg, PA: Destiny Image, 2009), 214.

6. See Exodus 34:29-30.

CHAPTER 11

Creative Love

There are many descriptions and definitions of God's love. The Old Testament often uses the term *chesed* to describe the loyalty and the covenant commitment of God's love toward His people. The term *ahav* has the inherent connotation of generosity and service. The New Testament utilizes the term *agape*, which becomes the most common and unique word for God's uncreated love. This is the love that eternally exists between the Father and the Son in brilliant glory. This is the supernatural love from above that is poured out into our heart by the Holy Spirit. The unending flow of pure love into our deepest core provides the dynamic force for all growth and all fruit in our new life in Christ. This love is the defining foundation of our entire life as the children of God.

Love Versus Lust

God's love is—like God Himself—powerful and truly creative. It brings that which doesn't exist into existence. In contrast, the "love" that comes from the world *(cosmos)* is reactive and destructive, rooted in emptiness and longing. Its insatiable appetite sucks the life and beauty out of its objects, like a vampire. It desires the valuable, but once it is fully sated, it leaves its victims worthless and scorned. This uncreative love is actually lust—a desire to be filled with the life of another. Because any source other than God is finite, it cannot indefinitely sustain the ever-empty lover. As the "beloved" is used up and becomes less alive, strong desire turns to repulsion. This is the pattern of addiction and abuse.

Amnon lusted for his half sister, Tamar, enticed by her beauty and kind character. Once he violated her, he hated her. His hatred afterward was greater than his longing before. Her life was ruined. Her full brother Absalom eventually killed Amnon in retaliation. In turn, Absalom ended his life in utter ruin.

Man is uniquely wired for vital relationship with the living, beautiful God. He has an innate thirst for the infinite. This makes humans who are apart from God the most dangerous of all creatures. Craving for the limitless, a person can consume all the beauty and life in the people and the environment around him or her. He must be filled, but cannot find fulfillment within the limits of creation.

Essentially, everything the human apart from God touches turns to rust, or dust, or excrement. This is the root of madness found in the rapist, the abuser, the greedy miser, the conqueror, and others who cannot be satisfied. They are attempting to fill a void within so infinite that all the universe will not suffice. Plunging deeper into this void, the light inside becomes darkness and the way out more and more hidden.

Totally the opposite, *agape,* the love-light-energy of God, is poured in vast supply into the heart of the children of God. This *fills* the longing for the infinite and *lights up* the life. Filled with such love, everything we touch goes up in value! Agape love is creative. It takes trash and turns it into treasure! Like God, it sees value where none is obvious. It discovers and uncorks potential. Agape unleashes the Age to Come.

The Future and the Peanut

Divine love opens up the secret abundance of the creation. George Washington Carver was born into slavery, but he became one of the great scientists of his day. His discoveries in the laboratories and fields of Tuskegee, Alabama, flowed out of a deep love for God and concern for the people around him.

One night he was accosted and threatened by a poor white backwoods farmer. This man had switched from cotton to peanuts, as Dr. Carver had recommended in his publications and lectures. Initially, growing peanuts had saved Ambrose Lee Harper from bankruptcy, but as more farmers did the same, there were simply too many to sell. Once again Mr. Harper was facing ruin. No matter what was said, he could not be calmed. Shaking his fist he shouted, "We've all been fools, and you're the biggest fool of all, Mr. Carver!"

Dr. Carver's gentle soul was shaken by the words of this man. He knew that many more were suffering. Carver went to his laboratory and spent the rest of the night in tears, begging God for forgiveness and wisdom. He began to sense the presence of the Lord. Leaving the laboratory, he went out into the surrounding fields and woods. The soft breeze refreshed him.

With confidence he prayed, "Dear Creator, show me why You created the universe."

The wind rustled in the leaves of the trees and it was as if he heard a voice replying, "Your little mind asks too much. Ask something more your size."

Pondering this response, Carver then asked, "What is the purpose of man?"

Once more the voice answered, "You are still asking too much."

Falling to his knees, he prayed, "Dear Lord, show me why You made the peanut."

The breeze rustled the leaves and he heard, "Now you are asking questions your own size, and I can reveal the answers."

Divinely energized by supernatural love, Dr. Carver returned to his lab and worked unceasingly under supernatural direction *for six days and six nights.* During those six days, he discovered hundreds of practical uses for the peanut, including cooking oil, soap, inks, candies, ice cream, animal feed, dyes, shoe polish, salves, milk substitute, paper, soil conditioners, and medicines. These discoveries created entire new industries and markets for peanuts.

This small, humble man eventually gave persuasive testimony before Congress that changed laws to favor farmers. Carver's life was a gift from God to save the South from economic ruin. From the humblest of beginnings, he counted among his friends President Theodore Roosevelt and Henry Ford. These great men would regularly visit him, attracted to the creative energy of love shining through him.[1] Love made him a gateway for the future. On earth as it is in Heaven happens in practical terms through one human life at a time!

Love's Power to Restore Value

The 1964 Chevelle Malibu SS convertible was a red hot and exciting car for its day. Rolling off the assembly line, it possessed fine lines and plenty of power. Putting it through its paces was pure pleasure. It could turn heads and take someone comfortably from coast to coast—maybe even getting some kicks on Route 66!

But if it never received proper care, the car's beauty soon faded. Without regular maintenance, its powerful engine would actually destroy itself. In a short time this beautiful road machine could end up as nothing more than a perch for a junkyard dog. Or be crushed into scrap metal. Such total neglect would tell us that the owner was ignorant of the worth of this car.

This is how many human lives are lived…the potential unseen, the true worth overlooked. Life in the fast lane comes to a quick and tragic end. As cowboys would say of a neglected horse, "He was rode hard and put away wet too many times."

But if a collector happens by the junkyard the story may drastically change. Under that snarling dog, the car lover sees the remains of the

'64 Malibu and recognizes a potential classic! Seeing its true worth, he gladly pays for it and moves it. In his shop, he carefully dismantles it, wanting to keep as much original equipment as possible. The fenders go to a specialty body shop where they are reshaped into pristine condition. He pulls apart the engine and completely rebuilds a 396-cubic-inch power plant! He reupholsters with fine leather and restores the cloth top. He gives it a beautiful multi-layer paint job with several coats of clear lacquer. The car is re-created as close to the original as possible, only better! This trophy now costs many times more than the original car, but because of love, it's worth it.

Appreciation and Human Worth

God's uncreated love creates value where none is apparent. It is full and overflowing. It gives rather than takes. Everything it touches blossoms and bears fruit. It calls the dead to life and confers beauty at an essential rather than superficial level.

Appreciation is a good word to describe the function of God's love. God's love raises the value of its objects.

Appreciation is defined by the *New Oxford American Dictionary* as:

1. The recognition and enjoyment of the good qualities of someone or something,

2. A full understanding of a situation, and...

3. Increase in monetary value.

Agape sees the good qualities, grasps the potential, and raises the apparent value of everyone it touches. This appreciation flows out of honor.

Heavenly Love Waves

The substance of God's love is found in the titanic waves of essential love that flow between Father and Son. The Father sees the Son with great delight and pleasure; He considers the Son worthy of all glory and all honor. All that He has, He joyfully gives to the Son, declaring that the Son is worthy of all the worship in the universe!

The Son, overwhelmed and delighted by this extravagant love of the Father toward Him, can only give thanks and praise. He loves the Father with all that He is and returns all the love and all the honor that exists to the Father. He knows that one day, when the entire universe is under the dominion of love, that He will give the Kingdom to the Father.

This goes on forever—the waves of love and joy escalating continually for eternity. The Holy Spirit flows back and forth between the Father and the Son sharing what Each has said, delighted to carry the good words, not seeking His own honor. The Father and the Son esteem the Holy Spirit as the best! He is the Servant of Servants, the very Spirit or Breath of God!

It is hard to wrap our small 3-pound brains around the implications of this Heavenly love feast. It goes on forever. The only thing that could make it better would be for an innumerable company of creatures to join in. Perhaps the original impulse to create humankind came out of the generosity of love. It only increases. Every human being, with the capacity to be filled with the Infinite, becomes a potential vessel for this blazing love that is burning in the fellowship of the Father and the Son.

The Infinite Worth of Human Life

The effect of shining supernatural love is the capacity to see the true worth of an object. When we live in love, we live in God. We see what God sees.

There was a crucial turning point in the life of Mother Teresa that became the foundation for all she did. As a young nun, she worked with the poor in India within the confines of her order. It was physically and emotionally exhausting work. After a particularly grueling period, her superiors directed her to go to the mountains for a time of refreshing. She didn't want to go, but they insisted. So she left for a holiday in the cool mountains and forests to the northeast of Calcutta.

Boarding the train and finding her seat, she gazed out the window. Just as the train was pulling out of the station, her gaze fell upon an emaciated and diseased beggar. He could barely speak, but she heard his raspy words, "I thirst...."[2]

In that moment, she saw—not the dirty beggar—but Jesus Himself. She beheld in the poorest of the poor the image of the Creator. She saw the worth of that one man. This epiphany of divine love became the fuel that changed history. Mother Teresa spent the rest of her life ministering to the poor as if they were Jesus Himself. Her zeal and convictions have guided many thousands who continue her work around the world today. The influence of this 4-foot 11-inch tall Albanian woman grew so great that she won the Nobel Peace Prize and spoke to parliaments, kings, and presidents.

Here is one description of this woman possessed by love:

> Small of stature, rocklike in faith, Mother Teresa of Calcutta was entrusted with the mission of proclaiming God's thirsting love for humanity, especially for the poorest of the poor. *"God still loves the world and He sends you and me to be His love and His compassion to the poor."* She was a soul filled with the light of Christ, on fire with love for Him and burning with one desire: *"to quench His thirst for love and for souls."*[3]

A friend of mine, Shampa Rice, grew up in Calcutta across the street from the compound where Mother Teresa lived. She had no idea that she was famous. Shampa would see her fairly often. Usually when she did, Mother Teresa would walk over and give her a big hug. Those hugs were impartations!

When Teresa died in 1997, Shampa saw many famous world leaders attending the funeral service. Only then she recognized how this small woman's huge love had influenced the entire world.

The Price Is Right

The love of God declares the true worth of every human being. As a young believer I heard it said that even if I was the only human being on the planet, Jesus would still have died just for me. At the time, I could not really process this. I think the statement was intended to create a deep appreciation of the disproportionate kindness of God and to increase our loyalty and commitment to Jesus. It never dawned on me that the Price that was paid for the human race on the Cross was the appropriate price.

The worth of a human life was defined by the price that was paid for it. God is not stupid. He did not pay an extravagant price for a piece of junk. In fact, Jesus was Jewish and, as a culture, Jewish people are noted for getting a good price for the things they buy! Perhaps God bought us at a bargain price! Do we have any idea who we are or what we are worth?

I am often stricken by a thought during times of worship as we sing to God, "Worthy, worthy, You are worthy!": *I wonder if He is watching us sing and is also singing back to His bride that she too is worthy and altogether lovely.* This is the fellowship of love that exists between the Father, the Son, and the redeemed!

Endnotes

1. David R. Collins, *George Washington Carver: Man's Slave Becomes God's Scientist* (Fenton, Michigan: Mott Media, 1981), 105-109.

2. *Mother Teresa* (20th Century Fox, 2005) The Study Guide for the film also references this scene. The cry of Jesus from the Cross became foundational in all the communities she founded. From www.frpaulnewton.com/ithirstforyou: "Jesus is God, therefore His love, His Thirst, is infinite. He the Creator of the universe, asked for the love of His creatures. He thirsts for our love… These words: 'I thirst'—do they echo in our souls?"

3. The Holy See, "Mother Teresa of Calcutta (1910-1997)," http://www.vatican.va/news_services/liturgy/saints/ ns_lit_doc_20031019_madre-teresa_en.html.

CHAPTER 12

Toxic Negativity

Internal Fires

Heaven is entirely positive toward you. There is a glorious and radiant love that burns within the Creator. These are the fires of life! This uncreated love burns as the essence of life within every fiber of our being. His love is the spark of life, the fuel that keeps us alive and makes us His counterpart, his appropriate companion forever. This is the great mystery of love between the Bridegroom and the Bride. We thirst for His love. We gaze upon it. We are filled with it. We *become* it.

Negative thinking and negative religion threaten the love of God burning within. Negativity silently and often invisibly poisons us. It's so pervasive that we often don't notice. We accept it as normal. It's ***not!***

God's mercies are renewed toward us continually. They are brand-new today and are never worn out or faded. His love and His mercies are glorious and energizing to our human frame. I may feel weary and dried up, but His mercies are **new** this morning! I receive the flow of the unceasing love of God and His undiminished mercies. I inhale them, I drink them, I eat them. Fresh mercies are better than a double espresso!

Inhaling fresh mercy, I exhale my failure, my disappointment, and my confusion! For my spirit His mercies are like the oxygen my body demands. I am in constant need of fresh mercies.

Jeremiah lived in one of the darkest times ever. His entire nation was collapsing. No one listened to his prophetic pleas. He wept rivers of tears. What kept him going? In the midst of his Lamentations, he wrote this:

> *The steadfast love of the Lord never ceases; His mercies never come to an end; they are new every morning; great is Your faithfulness* (Lamentations 3:22-23 ESV).

Fresh mercy is the air that my soul—my personality—breathes! We need continual fresh love by design. His steadfast love, His *chesed*, cannot leave me. His mercies, His *rachamim* or tender compassions, are endless. They are the atmosphere of Heaven, as vast as the sky.

Selah. Take a break now.

Are you present? Are you enjoying this very moment?

Now **inhale** all the covenant love and loyalty you need!

Now **exhale** all the failure, disappointment, and offense that may have accumulated in your life in the past.

This is good for you. It will improve your personality.

You simply are not designed to live in a world without love! Your DNA, the divine design for your life, requires fresh mercies and steadfast love as a continual atmosphere. Providentially, you can carry this atmosphere with you anywhere you go and create your own internal weather system. As a New Creation, your windows open to Paradise. There is a capacity in your soul that converts God's love into power for living. You can be strengthened by fresh mercies. Faith works by love! Love catalyzes the power of faith.

Jeremiah was a great poet. His Hebrew language is remarkable. We can also translate his words this way:

> *Through the Lord's mercies we are not consumed, because His compassions fail not* (Lamentations 3:22 NKJV).

You cannot exist without the continual processing of God's love and mercies. It is *through* the Lord's mercies that we are not consumed. Like oxygen, they keep us alive!

The Invisible Poison

Our bodies teach us many lessons. Every cell in your body that uses energy is filled with wonderful tiny structures called mitochondria. These are the furnaces of your cells where oxygen combines with the nutrients from your food. The energy and warmth in your body comes from millions upon millions of these little power generators. All they need is oxygen to operate. However they can be shut down and destroyed by an unseen poison breathed in as easily as oxygen. This poison is carbon monoxide.

Negativity is as toxic to your soul as carbon monoxide (CO) is to your body's cells. Carbon monoxide is an odorless, invisible gas that puts the cells of our bodies into a stupor resulting in death. This poison is produced by the *partial combustion* of carbon in environments with restricted oxygen. Carbon monoxide is particularly "sticky" to your system.

In your red corpuscles, each molecule of hemoglobin normally can normally carry up to four molecules of oxygen (O_2) through your blood stream to the waiting cells. However, if even one molecule of CO is present among 240 molecules of O_2, it will attach to the hemoglobin. Once CO attaches, the hemoglobin becomes "lazy" and will no longer pick up any oxygen. Not only that, but in a normal environment, the CO stays attached to the hemoglobin for the lifespan of the corpuscle! It destroys the capacity of the red blood cells to work. CO is inert, meaning that once it is attached it just sits there.

Negative religion forms spiritual poison in an environment of restricted mercies. Living in a broken world, many sincere people are susceptible to negative religion and freely accept accusations and heavy loads of legalism. Continual feelings of inadequacy leave them sad and powerless. These poison their spirit and sap their personalities of the joy that gives them strength!

With a slight exposure, the symptoms of CO poisoning are fatigue, dizziness, headache, depression, and confusion. Long-term exposure to slight levels of this poison causes damage to the nervous system and brain. On the other hand, carbon dioxide (CO_2) is the product of full combustion. It is sensed by your body and exhaled.

Negativity does similar things to our spiritual lives as CO does to our bodies. No wonder so many precious believers are tired, confused, and depressed! Inert legalistic religion poisons with a lethal sense of condemnation.

In contrast, fresh mercies result in true conviction. Like normal CO_2, which causes us to exhale and be free, true conviction produces confession and repentance, which frees us from sin. We are purged of unrighteousness, and totally forgiven. The result is freedom and energy!

Open the windows of your soul! Let the fresh breezes of God's love and endless mercies change your inner atmosphere! Take huge, deep breaths of His great faithfulness! Set the tone of your day and the metabolic rate of your life with this simple routine:

Breathe in mercy with each breath. Exhale everything negative. You can't live without breath. To stay abundantly alive, you need His fresh mercies every morning!

A friend of mine who is a fire captain for the city of Baltimore told me that firefighters are regularly exposed to harmful amounts of carbon monoxide while fighting fires, even when wearing oxygen tanks and protective masks. When they come out of a fire for a break, someone who has not been in the burning structure will sniff the skin of the firefighter's face. If they detect the smell of smoke, they know that they have been inadvertently exposed to deadly carbon monoxide. Under normal conditions, it can take several weeks for the poisoned blood cells to be replaced by healthy corpuscles. During this time, the fire-fighters are not able to work. They are at risk for long-term damages to their health.

In order to return these brave men and women to active status sooner and to ensure their long-term health, they are placed in *oxygen-enriched hyperbaric chambers* (similar to decompression chambers used for deep sea divers) for several hours. In those chambers, under the pressure of several normal atmospheres, the lungs are so filled with oxygen that the cells will actually release the CO and receive the O_2!

The Hebrew word for *glory* can mean "weight" or "pressure." Many believers are inadvertently exposed to negativity. There is a faint smell of condemnation and discouragement on their faces. Quick! Get them into the glory! One of the best cures for toxic negativity is to soak in the glory of God for extended periods of time. In that atmosphere, God's kindness and power fills our beings with Light! Hyperbaric glory-love saturation will have you up and better than ever before you know it!

This is a good place to take another break and inhale some fresh new mercies! Let goodness overwhelm and replace all the negativity. His thoughts toward you are good! He has plans to prosper you and to give you a hope and a future!

Connection and Radiance

We are the brightly burning vessels of God's love for the world. God is love. There is nothing about His being or His actions that is not love. He is light, and in Him is no darkness at all. He is so completely love that He even loves His enemies. That's what He teaches us to do. In this, we learn by example. We mimic or follow His lead. It's how we grow into mature sons and daughters.

Even before I was a believer, I had heard that:

God so loved the world that He gave His one and only Son, that whoever believes in Him shall not perish but have eternal life (John 3:16).

The "world" is the system that is antagonistic toward God. God answers this intense and fundamental hatred with exquisite and unimaginable generosity. He gives the finest Gift in the universe. This is the way of God, and we are His true and genuine offspring. Despite His love, the world system hates Him, and we are not to be surprised when it hates us as well.[1] In response to that hatred, in the midst of gloom and negativity, we are cheerily commanded, "Rise and shine, boys and girls!" Remember your Daddy!

The question is: Is this possible? How can we keep burning with the love of God? Like supernatural light bulbs, we burn but are not consumed in the burning. We are designed as "super long-life" bulbs.

 There is a light bulb (shown to the left) that has been burning for over 100 years at a fire station in Livermore, California (about 50 miles west of San Francisco). That is the longest burn of any light bulb.[2] Sometime it will fail, but our light will not.

For a bulb to burn, it has to be connected to a complete power circuit. I like to raise my arms and point two fingers on each hand as if they were plugs. I plug one hand into the Father and one hand I plug into the Son. The current that flows through me is the Holy Spirit carrying the eternal, unlimited love of the Father for the Son. Then it flows back with the love of the Son for the Father! It's holy alternating current. When I am plugged into this circuit, I shine like the sun! This is the Radiant Glory!

Radiant love shifts the weather patterns of history and culture. Our shining is the translation of God's love into the needs of the world around us. It brings joy where there is despair. It brings forgiveness where it seems impossible. It sets us on the course of freedom. It is practical and full of good works.

The Power of Appreciation

Jaime Escalante, a Bolivian immigrant, taught mathematics at Garfield High School from 1974 to 1991. In a rough neighborhood of

East Los Angeles, he transformed the entire concept of what disadvantaged students could do when offered the opportunity to excel. You may have seen the movie *Stand and Deliver* based on his Advanced Placement calculus classes.

Mr. Escalante tells this story of a teacher who had two Johnny's in his class. They couldn't have been more different. One Johnny was an excellent student, a clear leader and role model. He worked diligently, participated in discussions, and was helpful to those around him. He always had his homework done on time. The other Johnny was sullen, disheveled, and unresponsive. He usually came in late, took his seat at the back of the class, and disrupted the class, causing trouble. He never had his homework and often was missing his book. After a few weeks, on the night of the first PTA open house there was opportunity for parent-teacher interaction. A large woman stayed after the others had left. She approached the teacher, introduced herself as Johnny's mother, and asked how her son Johnny was doing. The teacher was delighted to meet her.

Assuming she was the mother of the "good Johnny," he sincerely shared his admiration for her son and made a point of what a great asset Johnny was to the class. He told her that he would love to have an entire classroom full of kids like her son.

The next day, the two Johnny's came to class. Something was different. The troubled Johnny came in on time and had his homework done. He was attentive through the entire class, raising his hand and participating in discussions.

Everyone in the classroom noticed this sudden change in personality. When the class was dismissed, this Johnny stayed behind. He approached the teacher. Speaking softly he said, "My mom told me what you said about me. I've never had a teacher before who wanted me in his class."

He became one of the best students the teacher ever had. A simple case of mistaken identity and a dose of unintended appreciation changed Johnny's life![3]

As we shine with God's love, even our mistakes can change lives!

Endnote

1. See John 15:18-19.

2. http://www.centennialbulb.org. Accessed January 6, 2010.

3. Barbara Glanz, Adapted from *The Simple Truths of Appreciation* © *2007 by Simple Truths Naperville, Illinois.*

CHAPTER 13

Boundaries and Boundless Love

Magnetic Glory

We are genetically designed to carry radiant glory. We are God's children and bear a "family resemblance" to our Father! Increasing glory is our normal spiritual growth process. We often think of glory as radiant power, but power is only a part of glory. God's glory contains His personality.

In the darkness, our radiance stands out. It makes us powerfully magnetic. It causes an attraction. Glory is not limited to the thick manifest Presence of God; it is also His personality. We are the bearers of the Divine Personality in the midst of a negative, broken system. Jesus made it clear that He has given His glory to us!

I have given them the glory that You gave Me, that they may be one as We are one: I in them and You in Me. May they be brought to complete unity to let the world know that You

Sent me and have loved them even as You have loved Me (John 17:22-23).

The effect of glory is a supernatural oneness with God and each other. Even the Beatles knew that love is what brings us together. Everybody needs the shining light of love.

All you need is love
All together now!
All you need is love
Everybody!
All you need is love, love
Love is all you need.[1]

God's Comprehensible Glory

God's glory is manifested in many ways. The vast expanse of the universe is a huge display for the dimensions of His wisdom, power, and beauty. It's huge, with an estimated diameter of 27 billion light-years, and expanding! With the precise dance of the stars and the quantum mysteries of matter and energy, the physical creation comprises a textbook on glory. The intricate molecular processes of living organisms, the grace of birds in flight, the explosions of color, the fragrance in flowers, the miracles of intrauterine development of babies, and much, much more all proclaim that there is an intelligent Designer of all things. The physical universe speaks to all who will listen.

Early Glory Encounter

As mentioned in Chapter 2, in May 1969, Berkeley, California, was shaken with paroxysms of violence surrounding the People's Park. The word on the street was that a huge confrontation was coming sometime during Memorial Day weekend. On Thursday May 22, the police and National Guard had arrested 482 people, including many innocent people who were in parking lots of stores. They bussed the people about 25 miles east to the Santa Rita Detention Facility. The guards (many of whom were former military police just back from Vietnam) forced the detainees to kneel or lay face down on pea gravel for hours in the hot sun and nighttime fog. No one was allowed to use a toilet. Some were beaten with clubs. Many had guns held at their ribs. Among the "dangerous folk" arrested were grandmothers who were simply shopping on a Saturday morning![2] (A few years later, the Alameda County sheriff was removed and Santa Rita Center was closed.)

With this experience, I was thoroughly disillusioned with radical politics as a solution to society's ills. I had been trapped and pepper gassed from jeeps and choppers. I had been confronted with bayonets and threatened with arrest. The street in front of my dormitory was laced with concertina barbed wire. Military helicopters flew overhead announcing curfew zones and other necessary information. The whole scene was surreal. I was "done." Berkeley was not the future. It was a bizarre anomaly.

I needed a new perspective, something to collect my mind and soul, to help me find a peaceful center. A plan soon hatched! I would hitchhike up into the high Sierra of Yosemite National Park. Starting from Tuolumne Meadows near the top of Tioga Pass, I hoped to hike the 70 miles through Emigrant Basin Wilderness area and re-emerge near Kennedy Meadows onto the Sonora Pass Highway. This would take at least two nights of high altitude camping in wilderness and three days of strenuous hiking. No doubt some of the trails would still be clogged with snow. It would be totally challenging and require continual focus on survival. This seemed perfect—just what I needed. Once on the Sonora Pass Highway, I would hitch rides down the mountain and surprise my parents in their home in the little resort town of Twain Harte. I was definitely an optimist!

Leaving on Friday morning, I was happily surprised by how successful the hitchhiking went getting out of the Bay Area and across the Central Valley. Somewhere in the foothills, the driver of a nondescript station wagon pulled over. He was a diminutive and pleasant man with thick-lensed wire-rimmed glasses whose hair just covered the tops of his ears. He was from near Berkeley and heading to Yosemite Valley. This was great! He would take me into the Park to Crane Flat, where our ways would part. I would head up Tioga Pass.

As we talked, I found out he was a chemist—specifically a chemist who, as a side job, made LSD. He told me he had several thousand doses in the back of the stationwagon. I assumed he was going to rendezvous with a dealer and get a good chunk of money.

To climb from the foothills into the mid-elevation pine forests, California State Route 120 goes up an eight-mile-long hill known as the New Priest Grade. There is an Old Priest Grade that is only about two miles long, but it is very steep and only the locals know about it. We took the New Priest Grade, which snaked around the ridges and through the ravines of these chaparral-covered hills. At about 30 miles an hour, we were rounding an outside left turn when we heard squealing tires coming toward us. The oncoming, huge boat-like car was not making the turn. Instead, it was coming straight at us! Through the windshield, I saw a frightened dark-haired woman behind the wheel.

I ducked! Then—Wham! Our car saved her from sailing straight off the cliff and down the mountainside.

In 1969, seat belts were not standard equipment and not used much even if the car had them. Without a seat belt, my body followed Newton's first law of motion: objects in motion will stay in motion unless acted upon by an external force. At 30 miles an hour, I flew sideways and struck the metal dashboard with the right side of my chest—which stopped me instantly! Other than the pain in my side, I felt OK down on the floor. I was aware that the car had stopped. I got up and, with some effort, got out of the door, glad to be alive.

It was pretty clear neither of these cars was going to be driven away from the scene. There were no cell phones in those days, so we waited for a passing motorist, who told us he would phone or flag down a Highway Patrol car.

Around this time, it dawned on me that being with this car and its thousands of hits of acid might not be very smart. The Highway Patrol officer who would eventually show up might have a suspicion that he should investigate more than the simple collision. So just in case, I got my backpack and quietly started walking up Priest Grade toward the town of Big Oak Flat.

A few rides and several hours later, I found myself at the trailhead in Tuolumne Meadows. It was late afternoon, but since it was the end of May, I anticipated a good three or four hours of daylight. I hoped to cover a lot of ground in those hours, and perhaps even to cross out of the Park into the Wilderness Area. However, once I started to trek across the meadows, I recognized that the pain in my ribs was only getting worse. Adrenaline had masked it for the few hours after the accident, but there was no denying it now. I had cracked a rib. Each step was accompanied with piercing pain. I was *not* going to be able to climb mountains, traverse swollen icy streams, and scramble across talus fields for the next three days! It was time for a Plan B.

I decided I would spend the night in Tuolumne Meadows, and if I wasn't strong in the morning, I would hitch rides down the mountain, across the Tuolumne River Canyon, and back up to my parents' home. The Meadows are about 8,500 feet above sea level and cover several square miles of streams, bogs, and open grassy fields laced between small stands of trees. In various places granite domes protrude vertically up to heights of about 100 feet, like miniature mountains. As I walked around, I spotted one of these domes with a large crevice on one side, which made it possible to climb. Climbing to the top, I was amazed to find that the break was several feet wide at the top. It had filled in with soil and a thick mat of pine needles. There was even a 2-foot-high fir tree growing on top. This was a great place to sleep. It was unlikely that a black bear would bother climbing this big piece of rock, which made it even more attractive.

I clambered down and brought up my pack to set up a camp. It was a warm evening. After I made something to eat, the sun was beginning to set. The sky was painted beautiful shades of orange and pink. A few clouds and the high peaks around me picked up the alpenglow. I had an unobstructed view to the west. High above the meadow, I could see 50 or more miles of dark conifer forests as they sloped gently down to the west. The foothills with light colored grasses and dark chaparral receded down to the floor of the Great Central Valley, which was banded with belts of color, signifying rangeland giving way to orchards and irrigated fields. Across the valley, the rangelands returned, marching up the eastern slopes of the coastal range. I could make out the twin peaks of Mt. Diablo and Mt. Zion slightly to the north and Mt. Hamilton rising 4,000 feet above the Santa Clara Valley. It was a sweeping view of this slice of California. I seemed to even see the Pacific Ocean and the fog that was rolling into the Bay as day gave way to evening.

This whole sequence lasted an hour or more. I was totally captivated and felt "at one" with the world. I felt I could both see and feel the curvature of the horizon. In this perspective, I perceived the size of planet Earth. It was very, very huge. I was so tiny—merely a speck of animated dust riding on the thin crust of this great and mighty sphere whose interior raged with molten and flowing stone. Thoroughly humbled, I felt only awe toward this spinning orb upon which all my plans and activities seemed so small. The turmoil and tear gas of Berkeley and the trauma of the car crash seemed far away and irrelevant.

I was beholding the glory of the Creator in the creation and felt very small and thankful to be alive. But this wasn't the end. I sat transfixed as the sunset faded and dusk deepened into night. I could see the Valley towns light up: Merced, Turlock, Modesto, Tracy. Over the coastal range came the glow from the great cities of the San Francisco Bay. Soon, my attention was drawn upward to the waxing crescent moon and the countless millions of stars that shone like bright jewels against the darkness of space. The Milky Way splashed as a huge swath of pale light against the deepness of night. There was Orion the great archer, taking aim at the red eye of Taurus the Bull. There was the Big Dipper, the great mother bear leading her cubs through the sky. But my attention was not focused on the handful of constellations I could name. The endlessness and depth of the starry display engulfed my mind and emotions.

I knew enough of the great distances involved to be stricken again by the miracle of this Earth we know as home. In the midst this great expanse of universe, our sun is only an average star. Within the sun, a million Earths could easily fit. Even as I had felt so small on the curve of the Earth's crust, I now experienced that the entire Earth was less than a speck of dust in the immensity of all that is.

The Heavens Speak

What I experienced that night reverberated to the depths of my being. I knew there was a God who created all things. I didn't know His name. I didn't believe the story of His Son, but I knew He existed and that somehow I was connected to Him. I can't say how long this encounter lasted, whether it was an hour or three hours. But it was long enough for me to weep and be overwhelmed and receive a message of God's glory from the stars.

Years later, I read these ancient words penned by David, the shepherd king of Israel:

The heavens declare the glory of God; the skies proclaim the work of His hands. Day after day they pour forth speech; night after night they display knowledge. There is no speech or language where their voice is not heard. Their voice goes out into all the earth, their words to the ends of the world... (Psalm 19:1-4).

I recognized that the heavens had spoken to me. It was Grace revealing glory. God was making Himself attractive to me.

The next day I hitched rides home and spent the weekend walking in the forests that surround my hometown. I talked to decent people who were kind and for the most part good. I knew that Berkeley was in its own world. I couldn't figure out what The Answer was to Vietnam or the U.S. cities that were burning down with riots. I had no answers for the assassinations of John and Robert Kennedy and Dr. King and Malcolm X, but I knew there was a God and that if there was a God then there must be some ultimate answers.

Relational Glory

He is not only brilliant and powerful, God is supremely relational. He met with Moses face to face in a personal and friendly manner. During these encounters, Moses beseeched God not to send the people on their way without His "Presence." God's presence was essential to Israel's survival and identity. Without it Moses could not lead and the people would be indistinguishable from the surrounding nations. It seemed that the Lord was waiting for this response; so He told Moses that it would be as he requested.

But Moses sought one further thing. He wanted to *see* God's *glory!*

God had been meeting with him, yet Moses was more and more sure that there was so much more! He was fascinated by his encounters with the Creator of the Universe. However, there was an essential energy and nature that was still veiled, and he sensed it! What was there behind the veil?

God's response was that He would show Moses "all His goodness." He would proclaim His name—in other words, God would reveal His complete character. Moses may have wanted more. He may have wanted to see God as only God can see God.

It is in God's character that we able to comprehend aspects of His glory. It is in our character and the actions that express our character that the glory of God is comprehensible to those around us. They may sense the energy or light of God within and upon us. They may even detect an aura of radiance, but it's *in our actions that the character of glory becomes comprehensible.* In that sense we are not merely carriers of God's raw power, but we are the useful translators of that Divine Nature into humanly useful terms, through acts of kindness and service to the needy. When you are in a dark room, you want a light bulb, not just raw electricity!

God caused His glory to pass by Moses. He protected Moses from seeing His face, but allowed him to see the backside. We follow God, but we may not be able to anticipate where He is headed. As C.S. Lewis wrote concerning the lion, Aslan, who symbolizes God in *The Chronicles of Narnia:* God is not safe, but He is good![3]

When God appeared to Moses, He came and "stood there with" Moses. He came in a manner that was humanly comprehensible to Moses. Here is the account:

Then the Lord came down in the cloud and stood there with him and proclaimed His name, the Lord. And He passed in front of Moses, proclaiming, "The Lord, the Lord, the compassionate and gracious God, slow to anger, abounding in love and faithfulness, maintaining love to thousands, and forgiving wickedness, rebellion and sin. Yet He does not leave the guilty unpunished; He punishes the children and their children for the sin of the fathers to the third and fourth generation" (Exodus 34:5-7).

What can we gather from this Glory that was shown to Moses? The following table makes it easier to see that the glory God revealed was the glory of His personality and character.

Statement	Impact
The Lord, the Lord	I am, I am. I will be, I will be. God is self-existent and both is and will be whatever we need.
Compassionate	He has a deep connection with us, like a mother for the child of her womb.
Gracious	He is generous and prone to granting favor to those He loves.
Slow to anger	He is not waiting to club us with a big stick. He's not touchy, angry, or dyspeptic. In fact, He is fun!
Overflowing in steadfast love	God is an overflowing fountain of loyal love.
Overflowing in faithfulness and truth	He is absolutely reliable in His commitments.
Maintaining love to thousands (of generations)	He actually guards or keeps that quality of steadfast love to many people and to many generations.
Forgiving (bearing away) every kind of human frailty and misdeed	He makes a provision to stay in untroubled relationship with flawed people.
Not leaving the guilty unpunished	Despite how kind, gracious, and forgiving He is, He is just and will execute judgment.

This breathtaking character that God has declared will be fully manifested in Jesus Christ!

The Borders of Glory

Only humans perceive the glory of God in the universe. We also perceive glory in others. We are attracted to glory. We are created to be glory hounds. Some seek their own glory, which is no glory at all.

When we carry and radiate the glory of God, it makes us attractive. It may not change our physical appearance much at all, but nevertheless, the radiance of God's love makes us attractive. With that attraction comes responsibility.

People are so desperate to touch and see glory that they will lose healthy inhibitions. Some had no inhibitions anyway. To stay in glory, we need healthy boundaries. Without them, the temptations abound to take advantage of those who are drawn to the light. As soon as you do that, you fall out of glory.

When people are so blessed by God's supernatural love light that shines from you, they may come and offer their services and their finances. Some of the offers are appropriate, but some are not. They will come, associating you with the Lord and giving praise to Him. Isaiah the prophet foretold that people from all backgrounds will be attracted to us:

> *Nations will come to your light, kings to your*
> *sunburst brightness.*
>
> *Look up! Look around!*
>
> *Watch as they gather, watch as they approach you...*
> (Isaiah 60:3-4 MSG).

The energy of Uncreated Love in our lives draws people to God's glory. How can we be certain that we don't take advantage of innocent hearts—or not-so-innocent hearts—that are drawn to the brightness of glory that is upon us?

We must know what we want. We want to live in the integrity of God's supernatural love! Unpolluted and holy, agape love is the boundary that protects both us and those who come to us.

This isn't for some far off and foggy future; this is right now, every day. It allows you to stay in the Here-Now of powerful Presence. It keeps your radiant love shining and unsullied.

The boundaries of our glory-life are the boundaries of supernatural agape love. Every relational issue in human experience is maintained by the integrity of love. The New Testament makes it simple:

> *The commandments, "Do not commit adultery," "Do not murder," "Do not steal," "Do not covet," and whatever other commandment there may be, are summed up in this one rule: "Love your neighbor as yourself." Love does no harm to its neighbor. Therefore love is the fulfillment of the law* (Romans 13:9-10).

Love does nothing harmful. It keeps the life-sustaining boundary that protects our hearts and the lives of others from damage. The only obligation is to recreate Eden. In practical terms, we have an obligation to use the love that has poured into us usefully for the benefit of others.

This sparkling essence of God nourishes us as a living flow. It is the foundation upon which everything in our lives is built and by which it is measured. This is one of the most powerful prayers in the New Testament:

> *...I pray that you, being **rooted** and **established** in love, may have power, together with all the saints, to grasp how wide and long and high and deep is the love of Christ, and to **know this love** that surpasses knowledge—that you may be filled to the measure of all the fullness of God* (Ephesians 3:17-19).

God's supernatural love is the basis of all supernatural living. It defines our lives. It is the environment we live in. However, not all spiritual experiences are genuine shining light. Not everything that is spiritual is the genuine love of God.

Counterfeit Love

Dale Alter, a friend of mine, like me was drawn into the flower child, psychedelic milieu of San Francisco in the late 1960s. Here is part of his life story:

> In August of 1968 on a Sunday night my best friend Terry and I were meditating on LSD. I was trying to reach the seventh level and experience Samadhi.[4] I had experienced telepathy, astral projection and had many revelations and visions from spirits. I determined that I would completely let go and surrender to "the force" that night.
>
> As I meditated I started to enter realms of beautiful golden light and felt myself drawn by the seductive force of the Cosmic Mother. As I became more relaxed and passive a voice said, "Om tat sat,"[5] as I beheld all the universe. I kept feeling more sensual pleasure and felt a oneness with the cosmos.
>
> Quietly the Holy Spirit whispered in my ear, "Where's the **love?**"
>
> I wondered if I was deceived because I did not sense any love, only sensuality.
>
> At that instant, I realized that I was deceived by the devil. Everything turned dark and scary. I knew that it wasn't real and I asked God, "Where are You?"
>
> The Lord Jesus spoke in a powerful voice, "I am the Way, the Truth, and the Life and no man comes to the Father but by me."
>
> His voice entered deep in my heart and blew away all my idols and vain philosophies. Suddenly I saw my entire life on a video screen: I saw myself lying, stealing, and hurting girls, and dishonoring my parents and my grandfather. I saw that I was full of pride calling myself an avatar.[6] I saw the ugliness of my sin, particularly how I judged others for doing the same things that I did.

I hung my head in shame and desperation, perplexed at what to do. Now I knew the Truth, but I was too evil to have anything to do with the Father in Heaven.

Suddenly I was at the crucifixion looking up at Jesus dying, his arms wide open. He looked right into my eyes and I was overwhelmed by love. I started crying and cried out, "Father, forgive me!"

The blood of Jesus washed over me and as it did, a thousand pounds of weight came off of my shoulders. As I wept, Jesus absorbed me in the Cross; I died and found myself standing with Jesus on the other side. I felt a demonic presence leave me as the Holy Spirit came into my chest with a thunk. I knew that I was born again and that Jesus the Son of God was the truth.

From Dale's encounter, it can be seen that angels of light masquerade as God. The distinction between the counterfeit and the genuine is *true love*.

We are the supernatural offspring of God! In this world we shine like He shines! The roots of every activity and ambition in my life must be nourished from the soil of agape love! All that we are—our deeds, our dreams and desires, the way we process relationships, and more—must be fed on what God is. God is love! He wants to fill us up with what fills Him up.

Endnotes

1. John Lennon and Paul McCartney, "All You Need Is Love," recorded on *Yellow Submarine*, 1969.

2. Rorabaugh, 164.

3. "Safe?" said Mr. Beaver. "Who said anything about safe? 'Course he isn't safe. But he's good. He's the King, I tell you." —C.S. Lewis, *The Lion, the Witch and the Wardrobe* (The Chronicles of Narnia).

4. A state of intense concentration achieved through meditation. In Hindu yoga this is regarded as the final stage, at which union with the divine is reached (before or at death).

5. Sanskrit mantra, which means literally "all that is." It is usually translated as "Supreme Absolute Truth."

6. A manifestation of a deity or released soul in bodily form on earth; an incarnate divine teacher.

CHAPTER 14

Endless Supply

God Without Measure

God has no inherent limits—unless you consider unlimited goodness, graciousness, love, and joy as limits. There are some things God will never do and some things God will never be. But everything good, everything that is love and light and creativity, God is. He is overflowing with grace.

Out of His fullness we have all received! Reception is the key issue here. Everything in my natural abilities predisposes me to work toward my goals, to strive to achieve. Sometimes that is appropriate, but not with gifts.

We can't earn a gift! Grace is *received rather than achieved!* It is the expression of God's generous and sunny disposition. Grace is expressed in the miracle of the Incarnation.

The Creator Became His Highest Creation

Jesus Christ, the uncreated Creator, while remaining fully God, without ceasing to be God, became what we are! He did this all in one Person! He did this so that we might become what we were originally created to be. For those who enjoy deep theological mysteries, I have included the *Symbol of Chalcedon* at the end of this chapter. It was the creed hammered out by early church fathers in October 451 near Constantinople, in an attempt to make that which is mystery more comprehensible.[1]

The Creator enters into and dwells personally in His creation! That is the substance of the New Creation! His overflow becomes our flow! Out of His fullness, we all receive! He is brimming with over-the-top Truth and Grace.

As we welcome super-abounding grace—this power-laden generosity of God—it is heaped upon us, one gracious blessing upon the other! The amount isn't dictated by the size of our need, but by the immense riches of His Grace! It's as if the Pacific Ocean is dumped into your backyard swimming pool! We simply drown in grace. Our old way of life is supplanted by a superior life coming down from above! This is the new birth into the New Creation.

We succumb to grace and drown, being plunged into a sea of joy. Blissfully we find that our New Life is safely hidden with Christ in God! Brand-new love creations, *"...in this world we are like Him"* (1 John 4:17). This is what we were supposed to be in the first place!

The Limitless God, absolutely infinite in characteristics and dimensions, made us in His image. Like Him, we are meant to live with unconstrained and completely holy love, joy, and freedom. This is the work of salvation. This is the result of *being fully possessed by the love of God!*

Planting our lives in the love of God, the taproot goes down into the bottomless depths of divine bliss and unending mercies. This is provided free of charge to any who thirst. No other qualification is necessary!

The shock, the outrage of Grace is that you can't earn it, no matter how good you are. It is freely given to saints and sinners alike. It can never be reduced to a wage. No! This is glorious Grace, unearned, undeserved, and completely infinite beyond our most ambitious dreams and darkest sins!

Anne and I have six grandchildren. Of course, they are absolutely the best in the whole world. I hope you feel the same if you have grandchildren. We totally get jazzed when we can surprise them with something that is beyond their expectations.

God's endless delight must be in lavishing this shocking, surprising, unearned, and totally glorious gift upon person after person! Each time an undeserving, warped, or reasonably normal but defective human is completely transformed by drinking *the free gift* of the waters of life, the angelic joy parties carry on wildly. It is the activity of both the Spirit and the Bride to invite the thirsty and the weary to come to the waters!

> *The Spirit and the bride say, "Come!" And let him who hears say, "Come!" Whoever is thirsty, let him come; and whoever wishes, let him take the free gift of the water of life* (Revelation 22:17).

To the world-weary, the disappointed dreamer, the childlike innocent, Jesus beckons in John 7, "Come to Me (and keep coming!) and drink (and keep drinking!)." He calls for the pleasure of our company. How exactly do we *drink?*

Thank God for all the scholars, scribes, and organizers! The Church has benefited by some of the greatest minds ever born. But thinking is not drinking! The effects are very different.

Along with our intellect, God will fill our emotions, our senses, and the core energies of our beings with His overflowing Grace and Truth! God's plan isn't to fill us as empty cisterns are filled with the runoff of seasonal rains. Much better, He will open up inner springs of spiritual potential, so that out of our guts, out of who will really are, will flow endless rivers of life giving water! Continual coming and constant drinking breaks open the fountains hidden deep within our wondrous humanity.

We are meant to overflow! Our thirst becomes a channel of creative and life-sustaining streams that flow from Heaven into the broken planet around us.

These living waters are the manifestation of the Holy Spirit—not just indwelling but overflowing through the personalities and activities of ordinary people who are now brimming with extraordinary potential. So filled with God that God Himself bursts forth from our inner being, we are Heaven's kaleidoscopic light show and artesian fountains of uncreated love. Consider this paraphrase of Jesus' words:

> Rivers of living water will brim and spill out of the depths of anyone who believes in Me this way, just as the Scripture says." (He said this in regard to the Spirit, whom those who believed in Him were about to receive. The Spirit had not yet been given because Jesus had not yet been glorified) (John 7:38-39 MSG).

When something is delicious, you may want more even after you are so full that it feels as if your belly will burst. I have eaten more than my fill of ripe, crisp watermelon. Even though I'm full, I don't want to quit. It's that way with the drinks we drink from Jesus!

The Holy Spirit reveals Jesus to us with such delight that, although we might not have normal thirst, we develop a spiritual desire for more. So, both by belief and by experience, we cultivate a strong desire for *more than enough!* We learn to stay thirsty.

A flowing river is always thirsty, though it is filled and flowing. It depends on a continual supply of fresh water to stay clear and healthful. In a drought, the springs that feed the river may dry up. When this happens the river can shrink into a stagnant channel or even a dry bed. Don't live below your God-given capacity!

We were created to be filled, and overfilled, to a degree that is called *all the fullness* of God! That is beyond human reason! What are the implications? How can the finite hold the Infinite? How can a water glass hold all the oceans of planet Earth? It is beyond understanding!

Only God can fill us. Only He has the infinity it takes. Only something that is beyond us can satisfy us. If we can imagine it, it's too small. If we can put it into words as a prayer, it's too limited. Most people err on the side of smallness, not largeness, when it comes to faith. Just try to exaggerate His goodness! He inhabits our praises—our wild boastings about God's greatness![2]

Fullness and Miracles

Our continual fullness releases the impossible into the personal and world situations around us. We are carrying miracles in our bellies. We don't have to know all about it; we just get to plunge into the joy flow of faith!

A life of fullness and joy sets us up for miracles. A couple of guys from our church, Life Center, were continually full of love and faith. They had developed a reputation for praying for healing. An Amish man who lived nearby, Leroy Peachey, slipped getting off a forklift on a construction site. He fell back, and as he did he snapped his femur—the largest bone in the body. One week after his accident, he was really miserable in his full leg cast. He instructed his sons to invite Ken and Fred to come to his home to pray for his leg.

When Ken and Fred entered the house, they saw Leroy sitting near the table with a hacksaw and a pair of tin snips. Leroy had serious intentions!

He pointed at his cast and said, "I want this thing off my leg."

Acting like old pros, they cut the cast off with a certain amount of apprehension. They prayed and asked him to stand. Leroy winced in pain. Acting like they did this all the time they instructed, "OK Leroy, now sit there and soak in the Presence of God."

While he was "soaking," Leroy pointed to one of his daughters and said, "I want you to pray for her. She has swimmer's ear. For two years she hasn't been able to hear out of that ear." They instructed her brother to put his fingers in her ears. Ken and Fred each held on to one of the brother's hands and then gave a simple command in Jesus' Name for the ears to open. Her ears popped open!

Their faith definitely went up. So they asked Leroy to stand and test his leg again. He took a tentative step. It still hurt. So they had him sit back down, prayed again, and told him to "soak" some more. While Leroy was doing that, he pointed to another daughter saying, "I want you to pray for this one."

My friends asked, "What's wrong with her?"

"Well, she has astigmatism. She's nearsighted in one eye and farsighted in the other." So Fred put his hands over her eyes. Ken and her brother held Fred's hands. They had just started to pray when Leroy interrupted. Signaling one of his sons, he said, "Hold that calendar up here." He pointed across the room. Across the dim kerosene-lit room the girl could easily read the number her brother pointed out—even every finely printed word! Nanny, the girl's mom, later told us that the girl threw her glasses away.

Now, with even more faith, Leroy pointed to a third daughter saying, "I want you to pray for her."

Ken and Fred were now laughing. "What's wrong with her?"

"When she was two years old, she broke her hip and her leg never grew out right," Mr. Peachey explained, "It's an inch and a half shorter than the other."

So they had the girl sit down. Ken held her legs while Fred and her brother Nate placed their hands on her shoulders. They commanded the leg to grow out in the Name of Jesus. And it did! She ran around the room with joy.

Finally, they had Leroy stand to his feet and try his leg one more time. He stomped his foot solidly on the floor. There was no pain at all!

Everything the River touches will live!

The River of God exceeds us, yet it fills us. It flows through us. Like rivers with earthen banks, this clear life-giving essence of God flows through us, infinite in potential, yet constant in thirst. We cannot drink just once, or even a few times, but must keep drinking.

Human life and virtually all life on earth involves water. We yearn for return to the River that flows from Pleasure to water the garden of life. How can we live without these waters? The history of individuals and cultures, nations and empires is written by thirst for Living Waters poured forth from the Divine Nature.

The Four Rivers of Eden

God is always on *full.* He is never empty or stressed. He ceaselessly brims over, not just in Heaven, but in our hearts with unlimited goodness, graciousness, love, and joy. All His goodness flows out from the Throne of His love. Creation is the fruit of the love of the Father conceived in God the Son, the Eternal Word who articulates that love and brought forth the universe!

The Spirit of God hovered over the formless void seeing its ultimate purpose: the human race. Once the human was created, the creature can behold and love God who is love. God placed the crown of His creation, *Ish* and *Isha,* in a protected place where they could thrive, a garden called Pleasure or Delight. We know it by its Hebrew name, *Eden.*

Out of Eden, out of Pleasure, flows the River that waters the whole garden of human endeavor. This transparent River of infinity dances with light and causes the garden to drink. It flows from the throne of endless intimate pleasure between the Father and the Beloved Son. It flows through the romance of the Bridegroom God and His Beloved Bride!

Genesis 2 says that as the River flows out from Eden, leaving the Garden of Delight, it has "new beginnings" and separates into four distinct headwaters. The River is so deep in creative potential that it becomes four new streams that encompass all purposeful activity.

Note: There is no place on earth where a river actually becomes four separate *headwaters.* These four "heads" are the springs of new flows. This is a *spiritual* rather than *geographical* river. It is described by the Psalmist:

> *There is a river whose streams make glad the city of God, the holy place where the Most High dwells* (Psalm 46:4).

Most great ancient cities and their attendant civilizations developed on the banks of a great river: Babylon on the Tigris and Euphrates. Egypt on the Nile. Rome on the Tiber. Paris on the Seine. London on the Thames. This is also true of most modern cities, such as New York City on the Hudson.

By contrast, Jerusalem only has a few springs. Yet spiritually it is a center of three great religions and the cultures that have developed from them. Clearly there is a River, whose currents or channels bring cheer to the City of God.

The names of the four rivers that flow from Pleasure with God are significant. The roots of their Hebrew names have great implications regarding the purpose for the human race:

- *Pishon:* to spread out, grow up, increase

- *Gihon:* to gush like a geyser, give birth

- *Hiddekel:* swiftness, like an arrow implying aim and purpose (sometimes translated *Tigris*)

- *Euphrates:* breakthrough and fruitfulness

Here is revelation of God's norm for human life, flowing out of unbroken and pleasurable intimacy with Him. These rivers that flow from our bellies hold within their currents everything we need to increase, grow up, experience joy, and bring forth life. In the River is clear direction and targeted purpose that swiftly flies toward its mark! Ultimately God has caused all things in the universe to cooperate for breakthrough and fruitfulness for those who love Him and are responding to the call of His purpose.

Living in Flow

There is an optimal state of human consciousness and performance that is without stress, anxiety or distraction. *Flow* is the state of champion athletes in their peak moments. We see it in the Olympic diver in perfect balance as well as in the quantum physicist cracking the code of creation and unlocking the secrets of subatomic matter and energy. It is the state of being in which artists produce their best and most creative works. It is the condition of scientists, inventors, and engineers when they achieve significant conceptual breakthroughs. In this state, effort ceases and the fruit of countless hours of preparation are birthed.

Flow is focused, joyful, and intensely "in the moment." It is here. It is now. Fullness flows out of this restful energy.

Flow is a manifestation of living in love. It is knowing that you are completely and unconditionally loved and always will be. It is feeling that same love radiating from your being toward every creature in the universe. You are like Him, complete and completely in the now. Flow is unlimited in potential and abounding in fruitfulness.

No worries, no resentments, no shame. Enter in. Drink. It is finished! Jesus said, "I have overcome. My peace I give to you. Be not troubled. Rejoice."

Flow is normative spirituality: effortless fullness is an overflowing life. It is contagious happiness, so saturated with uncreated love, so scented of Heaven, that every step drips, splashes, and exudes Life. We are the solution that the entire creation is eagerly anticipating. We carry this freedom within our bellies—which are ambulatory portals of Paradise! Can you feel the giggle rising up from within?

By contrast, many of our neighbors and colleagues have a view of "church people" as uptight, irrelevant, and boring. Sadly, that reputation has been at least partially earned by experiences with the same. But this is not true of living in the pure flow of joy that is our birthright! It's not true of the living Body. It is only true when the sons and daughters of God live disconnected from the Head, distanced from our Dayspring, replacing intimate friendship with rules and ethical regulations. Just a note here: Ethics are good and noble. But the entire ethic of the New Creation is summed up in this one command, "Love your neighbor *as* yourself." That deserves its own book!

Orchard of Life

The River waters the orchard of life.

We are created to be fruitful. Fruitful. Just think about fruit. Almost everyone likes fruit. Many kids—and even a few presidents—don't like vegetables. I think it's because of bad cooking, but that's a different subject altogether. Almost universally, people are attracted to fresh, ripe, juicy fruit.

Fruit is amazing. It's generally sweet, fragrant, tasty, colorful, and attractive. Fruit comes in a kaleidoscopic array of colors and hues. It can be sweet or tart, mild or intense, or just indescribably delicious. And fruit has seeds, the blueprint of the future. (Seedless fruit does not normally occur in nature.)

It's just plain fun to be around fruit. It's like dessert growing on a tree. Even the lowly strawberry plant can start a party! In at least one form, almost everyone in the world feels happy around fruit! In addition to being delicious, it's incredibly nutritious!

Dr. Mary Olney was an amazing and famous pediatrician, who saved many lives through her nutritional discoveries. She was also Anne's family doctor in San Francisco. She liked fruit, but once told me, "Fruit juice is one of the most pernicious habits ever developed." She thought eating fruit was much better than drinking its juice, because it lacked the fiber and other components found in the whole fruit. I think her view was extreme. Most people won't object to what happens when fruit is squeezed or puréed. It's still healthful and delicious!

It is totally normal for Christians to have plenty of fruit, in fact abundant fruit. We might ask ourselves when the last time was that just our presence started a party. Let's take some time to taste and see how juicy and good we are. Ask yourself, "Am I overflowing with tasty, sweet fragrant nutrition?" When we are fruitful, our Father is glorified!

Dried up Christians have put off more than a few people from joining the frolic and fun in the Father's House. Have you ever been disappointed to peel an orange and find that the insides were dry and tasteless? Have you bitten into an apple only to discover that instead of crisp, sweet, and tart, it was soft, mealy, and bland?

When we were kids, our family would drive down into the heat of the Central Valley to visit peach orchards near Modesto. Our mom would bring home lug boxes of huge tree-ripened peaches for canning. While she was canning, my four brothers and I had a sticky feast of as many of the peaches as we could nab before they were preserved. They were so sweet and juicy that the best way to eat them was outside and in our swimsuits. When we were done, we could hose off the damage!

Fullness and Flow water our lives with Heaven's personality! When our roots are deep in love, the fruit is juicy and sweet. I want to be dripping with the juicy and nutritious overflow of Heaven, affecting everything and everyone who partakes of my presence.

When we are *filled with the Spirit,* fruit happens! Like Flow, fruit is not something we work at—it's the normal produce of living in love. It's very rewarding.

> *My soul will be satisfied as with fat and rich food, and my mouth will praise You with joyful lips, when I remember You upon my bed, and meditate on You in the watches of the night; for You have been my help, and in the shadow of Your wings I will sing for joy* (Psalm 63:5-7 ESV).

Here is the key to true satisfaction and real fullness.

Endnote

1. Creed of Chalcedon from *Creeds of Christendom* by Phillip Schaff, public domain. "We, then, following the holy Fathers, all with one consent, teach men to confess one and the same Son, our Lord Jesus Christ, the same perfect in Godhead and also perfect in manhood; truly God and truly man, of a reasonable [rational] soul and body; consubstantial [coessential] with the Father according to the Godhead, and consubstantial with us according to the Manhood; in all things like unto us,

without sin; begotten before all ages of the Father according to the Godhead, and in these latter days, for us and for our salvation, born of the Virgin Mary, the Mother of God, according to the Manhood; one and the same Christ, Son, Lord, Only-begotten, to be acknowledged in two natures, *inconfusedly, unchangeably, indivisibly, inseparably;* the distinction of natures being by no means taken away by the union, but rather the property of each nature being preserved, and concurring in one Person and one Subsistence, not parted or divided into two persons, but one and the same Son, and only begotten, God the Word, the Lord Jesus Christ, as the prophets from the beginning [have declared] concerning him, and the Lord Jesus Christ himself has taught us, and the Creed of the holy Fathers has handed down to us."

2. See Ephesians 3:18-21.

CHAPTER 15

Taste and See

This chapter is an interlude intended for joy and devotion. Each section is a contemplation of one of the fruits of the Spirit. Each is intended as a Selah, a time to stop and let it sink in.

If you wish to hurry and finish the book, you may want to just look at the titles of the various pages or skip to the next chapter without even looking.

When you are in the mood, come back and use each fruit of the Spirit as a launching pad for refreshing and filling up with the sweet juicy fruit of the Spirit. For maximum benefit, I recommend that you slow down and only tackle one or two fruit flavors each day.

Take time to soak and saturate in the goodness of God. All these fruit make a great marinade for your daily offering of a living sacrifice! Enjoy!

A Brief Background

The Galatians started out well. Paul and Barnabas reached them with the revolutionary message of the love of God on Paul's first missionary journey. These Galatian believers had seen miraculous power and received the free gift of God's abounding Grace. The life of grace was revolutionary and totally different than anything they had ever seen or heard.

Shortly after Paul left, the "bad news" gang showed up and subverted the believers into a mixture of works and grace. Like children without parental guidance, they were duped. It seemed more reasonable that to really make God happy, they needed to work hard, keep some rules, and make some sacrifices. They adopted a form of Judaism mixed with the Gospel. Some were even being circumcised—no doubt a demotivator to the men!

When news reached Paul that his spiritual children had been bewitched by a false gospel, he was furious. You can feel his passion in the strong language he uses. His passionate concern was the occasion of the divine inspiration of this amazing revelation of the power of Grace.

He makes a pointed contrast between the destructive works of the flesh (the result of human effort) and the delightful fruit of the Holy Spirit that grows from abiding in the Spirit of God, drinking in the Grace that is always more than enough.

Let's plunge into this heavenly orchard and enjoy the fruit! Each is exquisite. You can never overeat!

The Flavors of Love

The fruit of the Spirit is love. This love of God is deep and boundless—truly fathomless. Within the love of God we find our native environment.

Jesus commanded—not suggested—that we dwell, that is, make our home in His love. There is never a reason to leave this wondrous portable paradise of the love of God. The Holy Spirit is continually pouring it out lavishly deep within our innermost beings.

This love of God is full of every nourishing and necessary facet of human happiness. It never comes to an end. This supernatural love is the soil in which happiness grows.

We take root in love, are nourished *by* love *in* love, and bear luscious, juicy fruit as we remain continually overtaken and overwhelmed by this wondrous Divine Nature. Rooted in love, we bear the fruit of the Spirit, which is love diversified, reproduced, and expressed through our unique personalities. Our personalities grow more delightful as we are delighted in the living, pulsing love which is the nature and activity of the Uncreated Creator who calls Himself Abba, or Daddy! As we gaze upon His Goodness, we reflect the world on which we are focused. We become what we behold.

Delighted, delightful, and fruitful, our lives are the garden of God, the Garden of Delight in which grows all manner of wholesome food. This love fruit is diverse and creative. Love's creativity is expressed in *appreciation.* Not only does love appreciate every person, but it creatively transforms that person, intrinsically increasing his or her obvious worth. In other words, the objects of love go up in value or appreciate!

The fruit of the Spirit are multicolored, variegated expressions of agape love, each with its own delicious flavor.

> *But the fruit of the Spirit is love, joy, peace, patience, kindness, goodness, faithfulness, gentleness and self-control. Against such things there is no law* (Galatians 5:22-23).

Are these nine fruits, or one fruit with eight segments? Scholars differ and I have no quarrel with any alternate view. The noun, *fruit,* and the verb, *is,* are both singular. This creates the image of something like an orange with eight segments. However, some people are more comfortable thinking of the fruit of the Spirit in the image of a cluster of nine distinct globes, like grapes. After all, Jesus is the True Vine.

Either way, it's *good eating!*

For personal application, I'm going with the eight segments of God's love, each with its own delights. The eight effervescent flavors of love are:

Joy! Peace! Patience! Kindness! Goodness! Faithfulness! Gentleness! And self-control!

If you blend them all together, you experience love, the nature of God. It's spiritual Tutti Frutti—all the facets of love gloriously complementing the others in a heavenly fruit punch.

For each of these tasty colors of love, there is no lethal overdose. There is no illegal amount. Although the Law was given to protect, guide, and make demands on human nature and culture, these juicy fruits of the Spirit are beyond the pale of the Law. They exist and pour out in unlimited quantities from the central event of Heaven, the ultimate Love-In: *the Fellowship of the Father and the Son!*

Each variety of love is available in the everlasting energy and activity of the precious and most Holy Spirit of God dwelling within us!

Bottomless Joy

Let's focus on joy, the first distinctive of the fruit of Heaven.

Saturate yourself in this unlimited joy and you will see the 3-pound human brain thoroughly drenched in endorphins, serotonin, and dopamine! This neurochemical state is a portable Heaven-on-earth experience.

Ecstatic joy is simply the *overflow* fruitfulness of the Holy Spirit *overloading* our inner beings! When divine love has reached complete saturation in our hearts and lives, the obvious fruit is *unhindered delight.* There is no shadow of sorrow over this radiance of glory that floods our hearts and minds with the joy of Heaven.

> *...Don't feel bad. The joy of God is your strength!*
> (Nehemiah 8:10 MSG)

The joy of the Lord gives a great strength. Like agape love, it is sovereign and not subject to external circumstances. Joy overcomes the outward and obvious situation. It sets captives free and can turn victims into more than conquerors. Joy is the intensely personal experience of being a participant in the Triumph of Christ.

Joy is commanded repeatedly, yet it cannot be manufactured by human effort. The command is really a command to *be* rather than *do*. When we rest in who we are, joy springs up like waters from the wells of salvation.

Joy is a gift from God and it is the fruit of His graciousness. I really like Eugene Peterson's version of the Bible, *The Message*. His paraphrases shock me with life and color I might overlook in familiar passages. In the story of Ezra and the captives who returned from Babylon to rebuild the Temple in Jerusalem, there is a statement that lights up my holy imagination:

> *With great joy they celebrated the Feast of Unraised Bread for seven days.* **GOD had plunged them into a sea of joy...** (Ezra 6:22 MSG).

Plunged into a sea of joy! That's sounds like surfin' on waves of light! Joy is good for you, physically and spiritually. It's beneficial to those around you as well.

Joy lights us up! Its power affects us physically, electrically, and chemically. Among the brain's many jobs is to be your own personal chemist. More than 100,000 chemical reactions go on in your brain every second! That's over 8.6 billion reactions in one day! This brain activity—billions of chemical reactions and millions of thoughts daily—is expressed outwardly in the emotional state.

The brain produces more than 50 identified psychoactive drugs. Some of these are associated with memory, others with intelligence, and still others are sedatives. Some of these are well known. Three of them really have an effect on your joy level and sense of well-being.

Endorphins are associated with the pleasurable "runner's high." These compounds are the brain's painkiller—three times more potent than morphine! A good laugh, extended exercise, or physical intimacy can trigger the long-lasting benefits of endorphins. Once released, they give an increase in happy feelings that can last up to 12 hours! Clinical studies show that endorphin production can also be triggered by positive thoughts. Time spent soaking up God's love every day can actually change your world!

Serotonin is a neurotransmitter involved in the transmission of nerve impulses. Serotonin helps us maintain a "happy feeling" and seems to help keep our moods under control by helping with sleep, calming anxiety, and relieving depression. Low serotonin levels are believed to be a main reason for many cases of mild to moderate depression which can lead to symptoms like anxiety, apathy, fear, feelings of worthlessness, insomnia, and fatigue.

Then there is *dopamine.* I think it is the most potent of the three we are discussing here. It makes people more talkative and excitable and is part of the feeling of infatuation or "puppy love" syndrome. In the words of the Big Bopper, "It makes me act so funny, makes me spend my money." Dopamine affects brain processes that control movement, emotional response, and the ability to experience pleasure and pain. All of these chemicals are natural and affect our bodily processes. These are the Designer's designer drugs!

Why is this important? *The fruit of the Spirit is evidenced in our expressed emotional state!*

These fruit are the produce of healthy rooting in the love of God, a continual abiding in the True Vine. I cannot, by human effort, keep track of all the millions of thoughts that fly through my mind each day. I certainly cannot control the more than 100,000-plus chemical reactions that occur each second! Even if it were possible, I would be consumed with the attempt to police my own being, fully absorbed in selfish futility! I hear the tortured Saul of Tarsus crying out, "O wretched man that I am, who will deliver me from the impossible demands of the Law?"

The solution is a daily saturation on the unrelenting overflow of Heaven's love, extravagant and gushing (more than 100,000 units per second) deep within! It is regulating and releasing the healthy, joyful, stabilizing chemistry of my own brain. Many of us could use more endorphins, serotonin, and especially dopamine!

A while back, I was preaching and spontaneously asked the Holy Spirit to release increased levels of serotonin and dopamine in the brains of the congregation. I was totally surprised when I saw the change in the demeanor of many of the hundreds of people sitting before me. Afterward, more than a few people told me that they were "blissed out" after that point. They were plunged into a sea of joy!

There is no law against this!

This is my prayer:

Oh, Holy Spirit, fill me, overwhelm me, and overflow my boundaries with the infinite Love of God! Let the unselfish and unlimited happiness of Heaven flow out of my being into every interaction I have this day!

Shalom—Nothing Missing, Nothing Broken

*And the **peace of God,** which surpasses every thought, will guard your hearts and your minds in Christ Jesus* (Philippians 4:7 HCSB).

Jesus is the Root and Offspring of David. He is forever woven into the human condition not only as the Creator of the Universe, but as the child and descendant of human beings! He truly is the Way, the Truth, and the Life, who returns us to the Father and to our true selves. He is the Way or the Path we walk in the great return to the Land of Promise. Not just Jews, but every human being is called to make a true, spiritual *aliyah* to the Land of His Promises. (That's a subject for another day!) We are only truly home when we live in the land of love, which overflows with milk and honey.[1] The fruit of that land of love is beyond compare.

The fruit growing in the land of love is planted by God Himself. It is heavenly fruit straight from Heaven. It is the juicy, sweet produce of the Holy Spirit growing in our lives. This glory fruit produces proper weight gain with the lighter loads of worry and increased weight of glory on our lives. You can never have too much! As you have seen, this wonderful fruit comes in eight wonderful flavors of Heaven.

The second flavor that delights the palate of our personality is ***peace.*** This is peace that is conferred upon us by the Root and Offspring of David! It is peace that is both superior to and in excess of every human thought. It is what Jesus left with His friends when He departed. It's superior to the everyday peace we find around us.[2]

Peace is much more than the absence of war or strife; it is the positive presence of wholeness, health, and completeness in every facet of life. *Shalom* speaks of every obligation fulfilled, every relationship harmonized, the abundance of the universe released for the benefit of all. The phrase, "All things work together for good" is a basic statement of living in shalom.[3]

So, right now, do this: *Imagine drinking a big flask of the fruit juice of peace.*

Savor it on your palate. Let it run down your throat. As it digests, it becomes you.

Peace gives us strength and courage in the face of every distressing circumstance. This peace is the original shalom of God that was in the Garden of Eden. It has no boundaries and can abide with us through the most chaotic experiences, assuring us that God is at work and in the end will produce Eden again in our lives.

Peace is personal and present. Ultimately it will fill the entire universe with the conditions of Heaven in which *nothing is missing and nothing is broken!* This is the bliss of the redeemed even in the "nasty here and now." Heaven is full of unlimited peace. Our simplest prayer is that God's will be done "on earth as it is in Heaven." (See Matthew 6:10.)

God's peace protects your heart and your mind from fears and from the common deception that we are alone and that our lives are without purpose.

How can the fruit of peace increase in your life? Simply, by consciously living in the land of love. Turn your attention to the endless love of God. Fix your mind on Him and become the recipient of not just a little peace, but unlimited, exponential peace. Consider this statement written 800 years before Christ:

> *You keep him in* **perfect peace** *whose mind is stayed on You,*
> *because he trusts in You* (Isaiah 26:3 ESV).

The Hebrew translated "perfect peace" is literally *shalom shalom.* This is the mechanism used in Hebrew to express the intensive condition. It is like shalom times shalom, or exponential wholeness, health, and completeness in every area!

When I hear the voice of the Holy Spirit within, I am the human channel of an endless fresh River that flows with the peace of God! The River of Peace flows through obedience. Its rewards are as vast as the ocean!

> *Oh that you had paid attention to My commandments! Then*
> *your* **peace** *would have been* **like a river,** *and your*
> *righteousness like the waves of the sea* (Isaiah 48:18 ESV).

This juicy fruit of peace is superior to and beyond any thought I can possibly think! This heavenly nutrition fills me with solutions to my personal challenges and to the problems confronting the world!

Today I'm going to savor every sip and every delicious, nutritious nutrient of the *nothing missing, nothing broken* fruit of ***peace!***

Love's Patience—The End of Panic

For no matter how many promises God has made, they are "Yes" in Christ. And so through Him the "Amen" is spoken by us to the glory of God (2 Corinthians 1:20).

We live in a jumpy, nervous culture. The phrase "tyranny of the urgent" is all too familiar and expressed in many of our daily lives. Anxiety and panic, debt and pressure, fatigue and frustration, alternating with boredom and apathy are emotional and relational diseases of our day.

Yet there is a cure! Within our inmost being a river of supernatural, uncreated love straight from Heaven's Throne is brimming over with every curative nutrient to treat exhaustion of the soul! The initial love flavors, joy and peace, naturally flow into patience. The energy of joy and the wholeness of peace give substance to patience.

This isn't run-of-the-mill, grim, toughing-it-out kind of patience. This exceeds "count to ten before you blow up" patience. This Spirit-fruit patience is part of the Personality of God!

The particular word used describes a passion that endures. Patience possesses a vision that is more long-lasting than the opposition. It cannot surrender to circumstances. *It recognizes no hopeless situations!* Patience expects difficulties to pass and the original vision to emerge. It delivers us from short tempers and quitting before the final victory. Patience is necessary to turn promises into possessions. Consider these words:

...Imitate those who through faith and patience inherit the promises (Hebrews 6:12 NKJV).

This is the fruit that is growing in your orchard! Stay rooted in love and the fruit will be luscious. This fruit sticks with the original purpose, joyfully and tenaciously clinging to the expected victory.

The New Testament uses a word here that denotes "a state of *emotional calm* in the face of provocation or misfortune."[4] Another definition is "a state of remaining tranquil while awaiting an outcome."[5] I like the phrase *"awaiting an outcome."* That's what I'm doing!

The nourishing nectar of patience keeps us focused on the outcome! Love assures us of God's best intentions. After all, He is the One who causes "all things to work together for the good of those who love Him, for those who are called by His purposes!"[6] Patience is the juicy, wholesome flavor of love that latches onto the assurance of supernatural love.

Patience keeps us free from complaint or irritation so that we can:

> *Do everything without complaining or arguing, so that you may become blameless and pure, children of God without fault in a crooked and depraved generation, in which you shine like stars in the universe* (Philippians 2:14-15).

Abram and Sarai were both getting up in their years and had no children together. Moses was approaching 80 and had spent four decades as a herdsman for his father-in-law. It seemed that life had passed them by. In reality, they had not even entered into the prime time! Their purpose awakened and their souls were nourished by patience! Their latter years rocked!

This is love's patience. Its passion cannot be quenched with the waters of adverse circumstances. It frees us from panic and the tyranny of the urgent.

Should you pray for patience? As a brand-new believer I did. A lot of stuff happened—some of it unpleasant. I thought it was great! I experienced the living God answering my prayers! Later, I was smarter about what to pray.

No matter what happens, you're going to need patience. Patience isn't passive; it's active and victorious. It's God's strength. So yes, I think it is good to pray for patience to so fill you that when bad things happen, they don't faze you. By faith and patience, we possess the promises!

Pray this simple prayer:

Holy Spirit of God, pour out in my heart the measureless love of God. Nourish me with the wholesome and victorious patience toward every good promise of God.

Kindness—Love on the Mild Side

> *Love is patient, love is **kind**. It does not envy, it does not boast, it is not proud* (1 Corinthians 13:4).

Kindness is one of the most prominent and nutritious flavors of God's supernatural agape love. It is relatively mild, easy to take, and fills us with hope. Human beings are designed to need kindness.

Kindness is defined as "the quality of being friendly, generous, and considerate."[7]

Kindness is the emotional and relational foundation for healthful and productive lives. The particular word used in the Greek New Testament is used to describe a wine that has properly aged and is smooth to the mouth. Kindness is the smooth friendliness of God's love toward all. He is never harsh, biting, or unkind.

Although it is smooth and easy to swallow, kindness is a very powerful aspect of love. The ancient Greeks considered kindness the peak moral excellence, revealing an inner greatness springing from true goodness of heart.

God is kind to all. There are times when you *need* God Himself to supply you with kindness! Just ask any young mother! Kindness makes us like God.

> *But love your enemies, do good to them, and lend to them without expecting to get anything back. Then your reward will be great, and you will be sons of the Most High, because He is **kind** to the ungrateful and wicked* (Luke 6:35).

Love's kindness makes it possible to nourish the world around us. Many are attracted to its smooth and nonthreatening character. Kindness is found in walking with Jesus. To those who were exhausted by the rigors of legalism, He said, *"Come to Me and learn of Me. My yoke is easy (or kind) and My burden is light"* (Matt. 11:28-30).

Kindness is the "easy to take" flavor of love! You can never overdose on kindness or grow weary of its benefits.

Kindness is far more than just being "nice." It is an expression of God's most powerful acts. *Kindness is the emotional expression of grace, overflowing into salvation.* It is one of the ways we receive and express the fullness of Christ dwelling in us.

> And God raised us up with Christ and seated us with Him in the heavenly realms in Christ Jesus, in order that in the coming ages He might show the incomparable riches of His grace, **expressed in His kindness** to us in Christ Jesus (Ephesians 2:6-7).

Let's drink deeply of this wonderful, juicy kindness of God until we overflow with kindness toward all! Kindness is the essence of God's deliverance for all creation!

Here is one more passage in which kindness is at the very heart of God's most powerful activity:

> But when the **kindness** and love of God our Savior appeared, He saved us, not because of righteous things we had done, but because of His mercy. He saved us through the washing of re-birth and renewal by the Holy Spirit, whom He poured out on us generously through Jesus Christ our Savior, so that, having been justified by His grace, we might become heirs having the hope of eternal life (Titus 3:4-7).

Oh, Holy Spirit, fill me until I overflow. Delight my senses and flow through me to express Your love on a daily and even momentary basis through kindness to all!

The Generous Goodness of God

Love is God's essence and activity. Our hearts are the soil in which the fruit of love grows without effort. It grows by the continual presence and activity of the Holy Spirit within. He is the life flow of the True Vine, who declares in our deepest being the conversation of love and wisdom going on between the Father and the Son. He pours out this limitless love of God, nourishing the DNA of our new nature and producing delicious fruit.

Kindness and goodness are at the center of a menu of fruit delights. Goodness and kindness seem quite similar. In fact *everything* about *every* other flavor seems *good* as well. So what special qualities are wrapped up in *goodness?*

Here are a few dictionary definitions of goodness:

- the quality of being good, in particular.

- virtue; moral excellence: *a belief in the basic goodness of mankind.*

- kindness; generosity: *he did it out of the goodness of his heart.*

- the beneficial or nourishing element of food.[8]

There are many terms that express moral excellence, but of all these words, *goodness* is the broadest in meaning! It describes an excellence so well established that it is thought of as inherent or innate and is associated with kindness, generosity, helpfulness, and sincerity! **Goodness is superior to virtue and rectitude,** which are acquired and scrupulously maintained in spite of temptation or evil influences. Goodness is innately excellent!

God is good and His goodness is poured out in our hearts. Goodness is the flavor of divine love that is altogether nourishing and beneficial. It carries with it *benefits* and *blessings.* Goodness makes us like God. Goodness is not just a noun; it describes the activity of generosity giving of itself, flowing from wholesome moral qualities, like a River of Life. Goodness delivers the goods!

Goodness is characterized by an active interest in the welfare of others. It comes not from our own self-efforts but from the flow of divine love released within our beings. It is both God who is good and God who makes us good.

In 1998, two women in our church came to me with a strong desire to help at-risk children who lived in an inner city neighborhood that was right up the street. So they went to work on this dream of theirs. It was challenging and demanding. They worked out a model for this endeavor, taking individual children into the after-school aspect of the program. One of the women had some significant changes in her situation that made it impossible to continue. The other carried on. She built a team around her and called the ministry "Center for Champions" with a vision of helping children to reach their potential through after-school programs and family mentoring.

Through the past ten years, they have selected children, helped single parents, run midnight basketball programs, raised funds through businesses and churches—and been cursed, threatened with weapons, and screamed at. But through it all they have not lost the desire to change the world one family at a time. They now have many success stories. Single moms have purchased their own homes. Students have graduated from high schools—many the first in their entire family histories. Some have gone on to college; some have started businesses. It has been hard work. It has never been easy. So what keeps it going? Goodness. It is the moral fiber of God Himself poured day after day into the hearts of this dedicated team. Through them, hundreds have tasted the sweet fruit of goodness.

In the New Creation, there are good works prepared for us in advance! (See Ephesians 2:10.) Goodness connects us to those good works. Goodness flows from the living fountains of the Holy Spirit, continually watering our innermost being with the liquid agape love of God. Goodness improves conditions and brings about prosperity to all those touched by it.

Goodness doesn't just flow *from* us. Everything good is flowing *toward* us from every dimension that exists! God causes all the good in the universe to target us![9] Just think: you have a bull's eye on your back for missiles of supernatural goodness!

In fact goodness, along with mercy, is chasing after you, ready to jump up and knock you over as soon as it can catch you! We are being relentlessly hounded by goodness! It won't give up![10]

This makes me jump up and shout "Thank You!" over and over to our Father, from whom all blessings flow.

Faith—The Reliable Flavor of Love

As we delight ourselves in the pure vitality of love, each flavor transforms us more delightfully into His image. Continually filled with joy, enriched by peace, encouraged by patience, we overflow with kindness. Those around us receive benefits from the goodness that fills us. Then we find that we are strengthened by a most nourishing fruit flavor—faith!

Faith makes me positive and optimistic. Faith is not wishful thinking, but a deep conviction within that when I live in love, I live in God, and God in me! Faith says "Yes!" to the promises of God. How can depression compete with that reality?

Faith is *substantial* and *active*. It gives substance to all we hope for. Because it is substantial it transforms the promise into an inheritance. Faith and faithfulness are indistinguishable. Faith and faithfulness are both part of the full-of-wonder love of God that washes our inner beings in unceasing waves of glory! The supernatural love of God makes us like God, so that in this world we are like Him. It restores His image to our personalities on a moment-by-moment basis.

God is faithful and reliable in all His ways. This wonderful flavor of love called faith flows from the root of love, transforming us and making us completely reliable.

> *For the Son of God, Jesus Christ…was not "Yes" and "No,"* **but in Him it has always been "Yes."** *For no matter how many promises God has made, they are "Yes" in Christ. And so through Him the "Amen" is spoken by us to the glory of God* (2 Corinthians 1:19-20).

Our faith in God is transformed situation by situation into experience and activity. It is living and active with all the energy and kindness of God.

Faith connects us to the things we hear. The Comforter is continually revealing to us the conversation of the Father and the Son. Faith comes by *hearing*. When we accurately hear the divine conversation, we are filled with conviction that the unseen realm is more real than that which is seen. We make ourselves at home in Him, and He finds His home in us. Faith is the fruit flavor of the New Creation.

Because He is utterly reliable, we can forever rely on what He speaks concerning us. His faithfulness ushers us into the true *rest* of faith. Ahh! I can feel my muscles relaxing and my aches and pains being soothed away in the gracious sauna of His love. I enter the rest of faith and find that I cease from my own works. His finished work of love on the Cross makes way for us to rest in the love God has for us.

The more we rest, the more He blesses. He shines into and upon our lives with glory beyond our wildest dreams. I find my virtue in Him and am caught up in His love for me. Faith assures me that God's intention toward me has always been positive. In Him, it's always been "Yes."

This glorious faith-faithfulness flavor of love delivers me from instability and haziness. Like Him, my word isn't "Yes" and "No," but my "yes" means "Yes," based in a divine positivity that gives me mountain-moving power!

Faith is full of the Divine Energy and is the working aspect of love. Faith's vitality is revealed in a steady stream of good works that pour forth from the lavish abundance of God's love. Faith is the victory of Christ within us that totally annihilates the opposition of the world system.

Take some time and savor the rich and wholesome flavor of faith that gives you such strength that your battles become the good fight of faith!

Love's Strength—Gentleness

Are you noticing a progression in these wonderful love flavors?

They actually lead toward ultimate Christlikeness! Love in all its nuances is totally beneficial. It cannot cause harm. Love ultimately frees us from the disappointing expectation that our rights will not be recognized and regarded by the all-too-fallible human beings around us. Instead it restructures our world view to one of an *internally renewed fullness.*

I can't be disappointed when I "imitate God" by pouring out of the fullness that I receive into the empty, broken, and needy human vessels all around me. I may sound like a pessimist toward humanity, but quite the opposite is true. I see every human as the crown of creation, the intended bearer of the Infinite and Divine Image of God. However, knowing that only some have recognized and received God's greatest gift, the New Creation, I do not expect other people to fill any emptiness I may temporarily feel. People often are a huge blessing, but they cannot fill me. God Himself is the only reliable Center and Source for the need of my soul to be continually filled. Sadly, many never learn this and spend needless emotional energy muddling and struggling through an existence of quiet desperation—or sometimes not so quiet.

Every moment, infinite love pours into my innermost being through the unceasing flow of the Holy Spirit. This is pure joy. Even in my empty moments and my dysfunctional actions, I am filled and refilled to overflowing with the most wonderful essence and activity of the uncreated Source of All that is!

The King of the Universe has set His throne in the midst of my being! This is not just an opinion or a perspective. This is an experience! The fruit comes from the root and my root is in the endless agape love of God. This is the fruit of the Spirit: love! And this love fills my life experience with the most alluring fragrances that draw me deeper into His Presence in all my thoughts. This overflows into my emotions and energizes my actions. These thoughts, emotions, and actions become established in my character and personality traits.

So what are the personality traits of God Himself? The fruit of the Spirit: love!

Joy and *peace* fill me with strength, energy, and a confidence in the abundant goodness that is pursuing us. *Patience* keeps me in the race. *Kindness* causes me to find ways to be truly helpful to all around me.

Goodness makes my life truly beneficial to humanity and the world. I will leave it better than I found it! *Faith* makes me powerful and reliable. I am both at rest and in the good fight to possess the inheritance that is granted to me.

The next fruitful flavor of love harnesses all my strength for good. *Gentleness* (or meekness) is translated from a word used to describe a fully trained warhorse whose great strength is completely under the mastery of the rider. Gentleness is strength that has been taught to respond to the will of another.

The bond between horse and rider can be profound and personal. Perhaps only dogs rival horses for bonding as deeply and affectionately to their masters. The human-horse connection is dynamic. Proper training can yield many measured gaits by which a horse delicately responds to the will of the rider. In a full gallop, the joy of the horse and the rider are one. The adrenaline and delicious freedom is intoxicating to both.

In the first century, the warhorse gave its rider both speed and the power of its own great weight. These horses raced into the battle and, at the command of the rider, were a great weapon as they reared up and came stepping down upon opposing soldiers. And yet, though possessed of great spirit and personality, they would exercise no will of their own that could endanger their rider. In battle, the horse might be cut by swords or pierced by spears and arrows, yet it had to remain reliably under the control of the rider. Anything less than perfect submission could be totally disastrous.

The warhorse had to be thoroughly free from panic and instincts of self-preservation. They could not "love their own life"—even if it meant death! One of the extreme training techniques was to walk the horse over a fire and halt it, allowing the flame to sear its tender underside. The horse would stand still without flinching. Such a horse was called "gentle" or "meek." It had become a trustworthy and potent weapon of war.

These same great horses that would race into battle could be trusted with a small toddler sitting on their backs. Each time they rode into battle, their masters completely entrusted their own lives to their gentle characters.

Jesus only did what He perceived the Father was doing. This was gentleness, a key to His great power as the Son of Man.

> *Take My yoke upon you, and learn from Me, for I am gentle and lowly in heart, and you will find rest for your souls* (Matthew 11:29 ESV).

The Holy Spirit's training in our lives takes us beyond merely being pleasant, agreeable people. He transforms us into powerful people who are clothed with strength, yet rested and refreshed in our inner beings. We become great warhorses for God, mighty in battle, fearful to the enemy, yet absolutely gentle to the weak and infirm. Meekness prepares us to repossess the earth, the rightful inheritance of humans who bear the divine image.

> *Blessed are the meek, for they shall inherit the earth* (Matthew 5:5 ESV).

Would you like to stop and pray this prayer?

> *Father, thank You for producing the meekness of Christ in my life, so that I may take part in the Divine Inheritance of planet Earth! Fill me, Holy Spirit, with this lovely flavor of Christ, that I might carry Jesus wisely and powerfully into the low places of the earth, bringing light, salvation, and healing. Amen!*

Self-Control—The Kingdom of God Within

The eighth and final flavor of God's supernatural love in this list is *self-control*. Each amazing fruit or flavor stands on its own as a facet of love, yet there is a progression. *Joy* is our strength and *peace* or shalom restores our divine inheritance. *Patience* keeps us in the good fight of faith with unflagging vision. *Kindness* flows out usefully to all around us. *Goodness* is purely excellent with beneficial generosity! *Faith* possesses the promises and makes us reliable.

Gentleness submits all our strength and potential to the will of the King of kings.

Mulling this over stokes my inner flame! Whoa, how He loves me! When I drink that in, I am radiant with light and overflowing with the juicy love of God!

Why would self-control be the final flavor on the list? We already have so much! Is it the practical expression of Heaven's well of supernatural love within? Is it the most exquisite flavor? Does He reserve the best for the ones who have already had plenty to drink?

Self-control makes God's Presence and Character credible to those around me. Self-control expresses the Wisdom of One greater than Solomon. It catches the attention of Heaven and expresses that Kingdom on earth.

Self-control can be as simple as not losing one's temper, not cheating on one's taxes or marriage, or just waiting until one can actually afford to pay cash for that big, expensive _____! (Fill that in with your own "could-be-an-idol" desire.) Self-control is the wait in "true love waits."

Self-control protects us from self-destruction. Self-control could change the world!

Self-control is the sweet love of God writing Heaven's constitution in our hearts. It is the mature expression of a life ruled by the perfect law of liberty.

> *Pay all your debts, except the debt of love for others. You can never finish paying that! If you love your neighbor, you will fulfill all the requirements of God's law (Romans 13:8 NLT).*

Self-control is *not* fussiness and a preoccupation with details. It is the righteousness, peace, and joy of Heaven continually governing our dreams, desires, and actions. It keeps us in the mind of Christ and sets our affections on things above.

More, Lord!

Endnotes

1. See John 4:16.

2. See John 14:27.

3. See Romans 8:28.

4. Johannes P. Louw and Eugene A. Nida, editors, *Greek-English Lexicon of the New Testament Based on Semantic Domains, Second Edition* (New York: United Bible Societies, 1989). Used by permission. Electronic text hypertexted and prepared by OakTree Software, Inc. Version 3.7.

5. Fredrick William Danker, editor, *A Greek - English Lexicon of the New Testament and other Early Christian Literature, Third Edition* (Chicago: University of Chicago Press, 2000). Electronic text hypertexted and prepared by OakTree Software, Inc. Version 1.3.

6. See Romans 8:28.

7. *New Oxford American Dictionary, Second Edition.*

8. Ibid.

9. See Romans 8:28, NASB.

10. See. Psalm 23:6 NKJV.

CHAPTER 16

Invitation to the Eternal Party!

We have come to the end game, the goal of our journey: a state of continual delight! It is for freedom that Christ set us free. The purpose for our liberation is to live in the perfect law of liberty, to remain in love all the time, not just to commute or visit on weekends. In one sense, in Christ we are home free before we even begin. Still many spend a lifetime working to please God and never enter into the *remaining rest of faith*.

How do we get there? We start with an awareness of *Presence*. Inside you is everything you need to be truly present, to be Here-Now. The Cross of Jesus Christ obliterated your dark *past*, lights up your bright *future*, and fills your *present* with limitless power.

Undistracted, freely connected to the endless affection and delight of God, you are the delivery system for the atmosphere of Heaven to fill the earth. That's real air conditioning! No condemnation, no resentments, no fear or anxiety, just pure joy and shining love. This is who you are in Him.

I recommend a daily practice of saturating or soaking your mind and emotions in the truth of His grace. Follow this dose of Heaven by consciously practicing *His Presence in your presence* until it just flows through you without effort or notice.

Remain present *Here* in the love God has for you right *Now*. You will glow in the dark with divine *radiance,* the love of God shining from your being. You *become* light, and wherever you go or stay, that pure-love energy radiates as the light of the world. This creative love causes everything it touches to *appreciate,* to go up in value.

Human hearts contain such desperation that neighbors and colleagues will be drawn to this love-light by tangible energy. Broken people will come to this shining with their needs, temptations, and traps. How do we avoid being sucked down the black holes of pride, greed, lust, and other dark devices? Roots hold us fast! Agape love spontaneously lays out wholesome boundaries and maintains our *integrity.*

Maintaining our integrity could be hard work if left to the hands of human effort and moral superiority. The streams of my own strength are fickle indeed! The Good News is that we are not dependent on our own strength. The artesian wells of *wholeness and fullness* are unleashed within. We are complete in Christ! We have been filled in Him!

Rather than carefully guarding my borders, I have the joy of nurturing the geysers of God's love within. The more full I am, the more purity and integrity fill me! The Holy Spirit sanctifies by His present flow through my life. Like the hot water pipe, I am only hot with holiness when the fire of the Holy Spirit is flowing through me.

That's not bad news. It's more reason for staying in love with Him with every breath I take! In Him I am more than satisfied with the pure bliss of salvation. In that bliss, I have no agenda, no neuroses, no manipulation. He is more than enough, yet He leaves me always wanting more!

Continual fullness takes me to a higher level—it takes me head over heels into the playful, delightful, romantic, and anxiety-free life that Jesus called Abundant Life! This is "life on full" rather than on empty. It is endless both in its eternity and its present nowness. This is the final state and the present possibility. We can experience our personal eschatology while still living.

Where the Spirit of the Lord is, there is Liberty!

Shabbat—The Everlasting Celebration!

One summer morning, I was sitting on the small gravel beach behind our house spending time with the Lord. The peaceful waters of the Conodoguinet were quietly moving, relaxed, and languid on their journey to the sea. Despite the tranquility around me, I was feeling exhausted and frazzled. After more than ten years of fighting spiritual battles, contending for promises, contending for the spiritual climate over our city, carrying "the River" to other nations, and releasing revival, I was just plain weary. I wasn't tired of God's presence, healings, miracles, or missions. I especially wasn't weary *of* the Presence of the Holy Spirit who filled so many meetings with tangible joy. But I was weary *in* all that good I was doing. And I knew that my condition was an inadvertent violation of Scripture. Just great!

With a fair amount of self-pity, I asked the Lord, "Why am I so exhausted?"

His answer was cryptic, "Read Jeremiah 17."

This wasn't a familiar passage that immediately gave me an "Aha" answer. So, with curiosity, I opened the Book. Some of what I read was disturbing, like this, *"Through your own fault you will lose the inheritance I gave you…"* (Jer. 17:4).

I'm glad that wasn't the "rhema word" to me! Other parts of the chapter were more hopeful and familiar. I didn't find the answer until I got to the last eight verses. It had to do with rest and the fulfillment of God's purposes.

Beginning in verse 19, Jeremiah was instructed to stand in *every gate* of Jerusalem and declare to the people that they had better take the Sabbath seriously. This got my attention. Something proclaimed in every gate of Jerusalem must be a really important message. The heart of the message was that they needed to honor the Sabbath. That's it. God sent Jeremiah to tell His people, "Stop conducting your businesses every single day! And stop bringing your burdens in and out of your houses every single day!"

I respect those who keep the Sabbath from Friday through Saturday sundown. I deeply enjoy the times when I'm with my Messianic friends who celebrate a *Shabbat* dinner in their homes and communities. Lighting the candles, feasting on the *challah,* and enjoying the Hebrew songs are all a huge delight. It's a window back to Eden and a glimpse of Heaven.

Yet I am of the personal persuasion that Jesus is my Sabbath rest. Every day can be a day of worship and delight. That summer morning the Lord was letting me know that my feelings of burnout were a result of being too busy and doing good things for too long. This insight wasn't just a temporary painkiller. This was going to be a life-changing revelation that would shape the rest of my days.

Let's read a little of Jeremiah's message:

> *If you are careful to obey Me, declares the Lord, and bring no load through the gates of this city on the Sabbath, but keep the Sabbath day holy by not doing any work on it, then kings who sit on David's throne will come through the gates...and this city will be inhabited forever* (Jeremiah 17:24-25).

The people of God needed to take a break. They didn't know how much. If they would just rest, then God would release the promises and the Kingdom would be established forever!

That's it!

Of course, there is more to rest than goofing off. For the Israelites resting was an act of faith. It was honoring God, trusting Him as their Provider and Source.

Underneath is a very radical concept: the good life, the promised Kingdom of glory would come—*not by* continual uninterrupted *work*—but by rhythmic times of *rest* and enjoyment of God, family, and neighbors. It was that simple. It wasn't keeping the Sabbath *plus*

612 other requirements. The condition on this promise of inexplicable divine favor was simply to take 24 hours out of every week and really take a good break! How different is that from our "normal" approach to life?

This message is even more astounding if we realize the very late timing of Jeremiah's message. These were the last days of Judah! The Northern Kingdom was gone. The ten northern tribes had been scattered by the Assyrians. This was a last-ditch offer from God to the leaders of Judah. God would restore everything and fulfill the promises to David. *All they had to do was rest!*

With God, *doing nothing* in trust and love is *more productive* than all the accumulated labor that is missed by honoring the Sabbath! Real resting requires faith.

What would stop God's people from obeying such a simple command? Well, for hard-driving type A personalities,[1] it is simple arithmetic. That day off takes a lot of time out of the year. If you take an eight-hour day and multiply it by 52 weeks in a year, you discover that the simple loss of those eight hours each week accumulates to over 400 hours, or more than eight 48-hour workweeks!

On top of the apparent loss of productivity, the concept of a weekly rest was not commonly held in the ancient world. Because it has been normalized into our culture, which has Judeo-Christian roots, we take it as a given. It is not necessarily so in other cultures. Truly pagan cultures that are untouched by the Gospel have a very uneven view of time. Whole months of days go by, each essentially the same. The only breaks in the pattern are usually for festivals at key times.

Even in somewhat recent times, the French Revolution and the resultant Republic attempted to throw out everything associated with the king and the Catholic Church. Eliminating the seven-day week, they instituted a system of three ten-day cycles for each month. One day off in ten seemed more rational to them. It didn't work. People suffered. Even the farm animals suffered. After 12 years the system was abandoned and the seven-day week returned to la belle France in 1805.

But back to Jerusalem: the prophet Jeremiah was crying out for change! His message was simple. These princes and prominent businesspeople just needed to shut down the cotton-pickin' store one day a week and let their employees rest, relate to family and friends and take time to worship God. The Sabbath wasn't just for laborers, but for owners as well.

I can imagine the pressure on an import-export business. Suppose a caravan from a distant land arrived a few minutes after sundown on Friday. The head honcho contacts the business owner to let him know that the camels needed to be unloaded so that his drivers can be on their way first thing in the morning.

The merchant now finds himself in an awkward situation. Maybe he apologizes, saying, "Sorry, all my workers have gone home early today."

The caravan master responds, "Well, bring them back! What kind of business are you running here? I've got to leave first thing in the morning to pick up a load in Egypt."

Feeling a bit embarrassed, our Jewish merchant fumbles out a feeble, "Hmmm…I can't really do that. It's the Sabbath. It started 15 minutes ago."

At that, the foreigner is a bit taken aback, "Aw, come on. We've got an hour or more of daylight. Plus there is a full moon tonight. Look, let's just get these camels unloaded. We might even try to get halfway to our next destination before we bunk down for the night. I can drop my price. I won't have to charge you for lodging tonight. Don't your guys want to work? When is this Sabbath thing going to be over?"

Trying to sound reasonable, breaking into a slight awkward sweat, the merchant answers, "Um, tomorrow…Um, when the sun sets."

Frustrated, the transport foreman just can't believe this delay. He shouts, "You dimwit! That's the dumbest thing I've heard in a long time! Don't you know time is money? I'm going to have to raise my rates if you want me to keep bringing you stuff."

You can see the pressure that might slowly erode the observance of the Sabbath. If its true purpose is lost, then it's just an inconvenience. The Israelites missed the point, despite the drastic warnings.

It seems Jeremiah wasn't anybody's favorite during those days. No wonder his tears ran like rivers. The people didn't listen or pay attention. They just continued on their merry way…until it was too late.

Like them, we can misunderstand the words God sends to us. His thoughts toward us are thoughts of peace and plans to prosper us and not to harm us. But we don't necessarily get it. Like overactive kindergartners, we don't want to take a nap or even be quiet.

The passage becomes more drastic. The problem is that if we plug our ears, we can't hear even the most dire warnings.

> *If you do not…keep the Sabbath day…then I will kindle an unquenchable fire in the gates of Jerusalem that will consume her fortresses* (Jeremiah 17:27).

God said essentially that if they wouldn't rest, He would burn down their city! That's intense! Even in the face of Jeremiah's severe warning they didn't stop. They must have thought Jeremiah was a quack. Their lack of response was terminal. Nebuchadnezzar laid siege to Jerusalem a few years later and effectively extinguished the sputtering flame of the dynasty of David.

(Much, much later, a Son of David would be born in Bethlehem, but that's getting way ahead of this story.)

As I read these words of Jeremiah, God gave me insight into my own exhaustion. My feeling burnt out was the result of years of unrelenting pursuit. I had been seeking the Kingdom of God, working hard at "the ministry" and at revival, carrying the fire of the Holy Spirit to other nations, and keeping the fires burning in our own church. These were all good things. But I wasn't resting!

I left that morning encounter with the Holy Spirit duly notified. I didn't sense that God was calling me to observe the Sabbath as a weekly ritual, but to incorporate Sabbath principles into my daily life, my relationships, and the way I approached ministry. It has changed my life!

The Joy of Creation

Everything about the Sabbath is both surprising and liberating. I plunged into a study of the Sabbath and found that it is a gift of delight. The Sabbath has to do with joyful, loving relationships. If properly understood and applied, it creates a culture where the Great Commandment can be expressed in lifestyle.

The Sabbath is part of the creation account. Creation itself flowed out of the love between the Father and the Son. He created the universe with glorious waves of love, light, and joy. Creation was pure delight![2] Imagine the wild joy when the first stars began to shine! Even as beautiful architecture or exquisite craftsmanship can fill us with wonder, the delight in Heaven must have been beyond exaggeration as the universe unfolded. Surprise after amazing surprise came right out of the mouth of God into existence!

Creation continued until it reached its ultimate purpose: the human. Here was God's best idea in physical manifestation.

Unique in creation, the human was made in the *image and likeness* of the Creator! Only in man does the creature truly behold the Creator. Only the 3-pound human brain reaches out to edges of the galaxies and beyond. *Homo sapiens* pursues, innovates, records, analyzes, and uncovers the glories of the physical universe. Only humans develop the fluid and intricate language that captures and communicates the experience of life! Only the human records history; builds great civilizations; composes symphonies; invents football, airplanes, and submarines; harnesses fire; and cooks beefsteaks and chocolate soufflé.

Humanity in all its potential was the goal of creation! The man—male and female—stood on planet Earth naked and unashamed, gloriously filled with light, destined to share the Throne of God with God, destined to participate in the Divine Nature.

And so God took the day off! He wasn't tired, but the work was finished. The universe in all its vast array was complete! So the Holy One declared a holiday that echoes through all creation. He specially blessed that day and made it supernaturally distinct. (See Genesis 2:1-3.)

This is quite a concept. The Father, Son, and Holy Spirit took the day off. I think they had a party! The glories of the creation process are hinted at throughout Scripture. One of the most provocative is found in the oral exam God gave to Job (who would soon graduate to a higher level of blessing). God asked Job if he knew how the foundations of the physical world came into being…

> *While the morning stars sang together and all the angels shouted for joy?* (Job 38:7)

Now that's a picture! It seems that as God created the physical universe, the angels were already there. While the work of creation was taking place, the angels and morning stars were singing together and shouting for joy! The morning stars (likely a high order of angelic being) sang in majestic harmony while the others were bursting forth with titanic shouts of joy that must have shaken the new universe. Sounds like a great party!

Even with all that angelic company, God was not satisfied. He was after a creature *more like Himself* than anything that already existed. The entire physical universe came into existence with one ultimate goal: that human beings would stand upon the earth and behold the sky *and what was behind the sky!* God had created a lover unlike any other.[3]

Now it was time to celebrate! So God took the day off. And so did Adam and Eve.

Can you imagine Adam and Eve watching the first sunrise ever beheld by human eyes in all its pristine color and glory? Never before had the Godlike darling of creation seen such colors and felt such delight as the rising sun heralded the potentials and adventures of a new day. Maybe they asked God, "What are we going to do today, Father?"

With a big smile, God's answer may have been, "Beloved, take the day off!"

They weren't tired. It was just time for love and delight. No wonder vacations and holidays are so important!

So God *blessed* this day of Shabbat. He infused it with supernatural restorative powers. He made it *holy*, set apart and brimming over with the energies of Heaven. Why? Maybe He wanted to dream about the distant future. Maybe the Father and the Son wanted to enjoy this moment and look ahead to the great drama about to unfold, the loss of innocence, the ransom Christ would pay, the ultimate triumph, and the great marriage feast that would lead into Eternity Future! We can't know for sure, but we do know that on that day…

> …*He rested from all the work of creating that He had done* (Genesis 2:3).

It was finished! He had done it! Time to have a party!

Endnotes

1. According to http://stress.about.com/od/understandingstress/a/type_a_person.htm,

   While the term "Type A" is thrown around often, it's not always fully known what specific characteristics make up "Type A" personality, even among experts. For example, some people, the term applies to rude and impatient people. Others see workaholics as "Type A." Many see competitiveness as the main characteristic. According to research, the following characteristics are the hallmark characteristics of Type A Behavior (TAB):

   Time Urgency and Impatience, as demonstrated by people who, among other things, get frustrated while waiting in line, interrupt others often, walk or talk at a rapid pace, and are always painfully aware of the time and how little of it they have to spare.

   Free-Floating Hostility or Aggressiveness, which shows up as impatience, rudeness, being easily upset over small things, or 'having a short fuse', for example.

   Additionally, Type A behavior often includes:

   Competitiveness

   Strong Achievement-Orientation

Certain Physical Characteristics That Result From Stress and Type A Behavior Over Years

Physical Characteristics: The following physical characteristics often accompany TAB:

Facial Tension (Tight Lips, Clenched Jaw, Etc.)

Tongue Clicking or Teeth Grinding

Dark Circles Under Eyes

Facial Sweating (On Forehead or Upper Lip)

Negative Effects of Type A Behavior: Over the years, the type of extra stress that most "Type A" people experience takes a toll on one's health and lifestyle. The following are some of the negative effects that are common among those exhibiting TAB:

Hyptertension: High blood pressure is common among "Type A" personalities, and has been to be as much as 84% more of a risk among those with Type A characteristics..

Heart Disease: Some experts predict that, for those exhibiting TAB, heart disease by age 65 is a virtual certainty.

Job Stress: "Type A" people usually find themselves in stressful, demanding jobs (and sometimes the jobs create the Type A behavior!), which lead to metabolic syndrome and other health problems.

Social Isolation: Those with TAB often alienate others, or spend too much time on work and focus too little on relationships, putting them at risk for social isolation and the increased stress that comes with it.

2. See Proverbs 8:30-31.

3. Before the foundation of this physical universe…the ultimate intentions of God would be worked out in the incarnation, death, and resurrection of Jesus Christ, who was and is and ever will be the ultimate union of very God and very man!

CHAPTER 17

A Culture of Delight!

The Divine Wedding Ring

One deluge and a few millennia later, God established an intimate friendship with Abraham. The life of this man, born near the delta of the Tigris and Euphrates rivers, would impact history and eternity like few others. He became God's friend. Out of his loins, way beyond the normal time of life, came a promised son named Laughter—or as we know him, Isaac. From Isaac would come Jacob the grappler, who became Israel, the prince of God. From Israel came the patriarchs. From these 12 boys and all their misery would come the 12 tribes and the nation of Israel. Israel would be the focal point of redemption history, from which the Messiah, the future, and the New Creation would spring.

On the way out of Egypt, every single Israelite experienced the miracle of the Sabbath. Once manna became their national diet, they found they could gather double on the sixth day, but none would appear on

the seventh. There was something supernatural about the double portion. On any other day, any leftovers bred worms and stank. Some
found this out the hard way.

On Friday night however, they didn't need to throw anything out.
What would have been wormy and rotten any other day was fresh and
delicious on the Sabbath.

Each week they got used to gathering a double blessing that would be
unusually preserved for the day of rest. It seemed that the heavenly manna
bakers must have also had the Sabbath off. Some tried going out on Saturday morning and all they got was sore feet. No manna on Saturday![1]

They eventually clued in. There was no real point in going out to
work on Saturday morning because the manna angels had the day off.
So Heaven came to earth and the people had a Shabbat—whether they
liked it or not. Some people are just hard to give hugs and kisses!

A little later, God declared that that the Sabbath is a sign of His love
to His people, Israel. It's something special between God and His chosen people. *In effect, the Sabbath was like a wedding ring given by God to
His beloved.*[2] Week after week for all time, as His people remember the
Sabbath, they are declaring in their lifestyle that God's care for them is
sure and that they are His beloved.

Vacations, Festivals, and Family Camping

There are many ways to look at the Sabbath and the great feasts of
Israel. They are treasure troves, laden with insights into Christ, Grace,
the unfolding of the ages, and much more. God gave the Law to lead
His people to Christ. Torah portrays the character of God.

The festivals and Sabbaths are a key to understanding God's personality. From a purely sociological point of view, they are fundamental
to creating a culture that models Heaven on earth! He never breaks a
sweat or gets nervous. God is love. Whoever lives in love lives in God,
and God in him! Far more than any human parent, God delights when
His children succeed!

The Festivals and Sabbaths are a key to understanding the nature of God's love. From a purely sociological point of view, they are fundamental to creating a culture that models Heaven on Earth!

The Sabbath principle reveals the joyful generosity of Heaven. Take a day off every week, no matter what, to love God, family, and neighbors. Relax, enjoy, and trust. God is overflowing with blessings. In addition to the weekly Sabbath, Israel had a floating "day off" every lunar month. Whenever the new moon arrived, everyone got an extra day off.

But just regular days off weren't enough for Yahweh's people. Their national lifestyle needed to reflect His magnanimous personality. In addition to these regular days set aside for love, there were the three great feast seasons: Passover-Unleavened Bread in the spring, First Fruits in early summer, and Trumpets-Atonement-Tabernacles in the autumn.[3]

These foreshadowed the Messiah and His Kingdom. In the simplest sense however, they were national vacations. For most of the inhabitants of the land, the feasts involved travel by foot. Three times a year extended families and whole villages went on community camping trips! Just to make sure the men didn't send the women and children without them, it was mandated that men in particular participate in these great national festivals.

Feasts filled with gratitude and adventure shaped the national culture of Israel. They required large groups of people to camp out, stopping to pitch tents, gather wood, and make fires. As they made their way up to Zion to celebrate God's goodness, the journey was part of the destination. Three times a year, every man, woman, and child in Israel would go on vacation! This is extravagant leisure!

Losing Jesus

We get a hint of the joyful, carefree nature of these times in the humorous (or disturbing) story of Joseph and Mary returning home from one of these great feasts. It appears that they were fairly relaxed in their parenting style.

When Jesus was 12 years old, His family went up to the Passover Feast. It seems they did this every year.[4] No doubt it was a great festival with lots of glory and a special sense of the gracious presence of God. On those holy days, they could almost forget the Roman occupation, the corrupt government, and other difficulties in their lives. Along with the rest of the faithful, this family from Nazareth celebrated the miracles and deliverances in the history of Israel.

Joseph and Mary must have wondered how their unique Son would mature and how His life would impact history. He was growing, and this year in particular He seemed to be showing keen spiritual insights. Certainly He would be ready for His bar mitzvah in the coming year.

Toward the end of the first day of travel, it was good to settle down for the night. Even on the way home, they had so much to talk about with friends and relatives. Perhaps as the sunset faded, they finally had a quiet moment together to recline and appreciate the stars beginning to sparkle. Still aglow with the sense of God's faithfulness and the sense of community from the festival, they may have held hands and caught up with the events of the day.

Joseph let out a relaxed sigh, reflecting contentedly, "What a great feast. I think this was the best year ever."

Mary nodded in agreement and mused, "I wonder what Yeshua was thinking. He seemed so intent on every word of the scribes this year. I've never seen Him quite so engaged."

"He sure was! Did you see the way His eyes lit up when he spoke with old Rabbi Cohen?" Joseph chuckled. "Hmmm…By the way, I don't remember seeing Him today. Did you?"

Mary bolted up from her repose, surprised by the unthinkable! "No." Her mind now racing, she added, "I assumed He was with you and the men."

Joseph furrowed his brow, thinking. "Actually, I'm not sure when I saw Him last. Let's see…"

They may not have slept much that night. How would you feel if you misplaced the Savior of the world?

Leaving in the gray light of dawn, they must have walked as fast as they could back up, up, up to Zion. They were going upstream against the crowds streaming down from Jerusalem. Oh, where could He be?

Of course we have the advantage that we read the story in such a concentrated form, but for them each step, each anxious scanning of clustered people must have seemed like it was taking just way too long!

Finally, after days of frantic searching, they found Him. He was having a great time "playing" with the sages and scholars, no doubt getting a huge kick out of stumping them or pointing out a delightfully original insight in a well-worn doctrine!

Upon spying Him, waves of relief, hurt, and parental frustration must have washed over Joseph and Mary! Here is the story in the words of Luke's Gospel:

> *After three days they found Him in the temple, sitting among the teachers, listening to them and asking them questions. And all who heard Him were amazed at His understanding and His answers. And when His parents saw Him, they were astonished. And His mother said to Him, "Son, why have You treated us so? Behold, Your father and I have been searching for You in great distress"* (Luke 2:46-48 ESV).

Jesus seems surprised by their distress. *Didn't they get it?* He wondered. "Didn't you know that I had to be in My Father's house?"

Spoken like a true adolescent. And like countless parents, before and since, they didn't really understand their bright young Son.

Were the angels rolling with laughter on the floors of Heaven at this huge practical joke? It's hilarious—or maddening, depending on your point of view.

Extravagant Leisure

These regular days off and generous national vacations were God's gift to His chosen people. Unlike any other nations of the earth, they were given specific revelation of the extravagant love of the Lord. The Law was set up to shape a culture of faith in God's goodness. The more they rested, the more they loved, and the more they loved, the more they walked in the ways of their Father. The more they did that, the more they prospered!

Even having the best vacations and days off in the ancient world were not enough to display the extravagant love and supernatural blessings of God. God had even more *outrageous blessings* to pour out! The Law *required* that God's children receive a benefit of staggering generosity:

After only six years of work, everybody gets a yearlong vacation!

What a Father! What a lifestyle!

Talk about luxury! How would this lavish holiday be paid for? How could any but the wealthiest afford such extravagance? By being blessed beyond measure! God said that He would supernaturally command abundance from the soil! For the same amount of work and seed, they would get two to three times as much harvest![5] It was as if the curse was lifted.

Imagine, for instance, the state of California or Kentucky declaring a one year vacation for every citizen. Try to picture Australia or India declaring one year off from work for every man, woman, and child. It's an out-of-this-world concept—with the guarantee that it would increase the national prosperity! No worries. Things will get better. Prosperity and good health will be commanded by the Creator of creation!

This Sabbath year was not just a once-in-a-lifetime blessing. It was designed to ensure that *every* Israelite, during *every* phase of life would have *a year like no other people*—a year to love, explore, worship, and delight in the bounty of their Heavenly Father's love for them. This was a year for the entire nation to live in supernaturally endowed joy, prosperity, creativity, and exuberance.

Even under the Law, our Father's grace was brimming over to produce a culture of love and delight! It's hard to wrap my head around the full intentions of this love-gift. How much more does He provide for us, who are not under Law but under Grace? Is it possible to exaggerate the goodness of God or the riches of His wisdom? I think not!

Delight Evangelism

Do you see how this regular experience of God's extravagant love could shape a culture that was like Heaven on earth? No worries. No poverty. No working to the bone. It was intended to be a lifestyle of holiness, kindness, generosity, and joy.

I think every overworked, oppressed laborer or slave, every careworn farmer or merchant, in fact, just about everyone in the surrounding nations would want to experience this! The sheer delight of such supernatural blessing would attract everyone to this Most High God of Israel! By foot, boat, camel, or donkey they would make their way into this Heaven on earth society ruled by loving kindness. Can you hear them coming? All the weary, heavy laden coming to Papa and His goodness?

It gets even better!

Jubilee and the Restoration of All Things

It is no wonder that Jesus focused His anger on the religious killjoys who had hijacked the pure joy of His Father's love! They had taken the ecstasies of delight and hidden them under sackcloth and ashes. Not only were the drudgeries of their traditions difficult and onerous, they were absolutely pointless!

The rhythmic Shabbat days, weeks of festivals, and years of worship, love, and play were calculated to produce a culture of unusual happiness. Edenic rest and happiness calls to us in these words of Jesus:

> *Are you tired? Worn out? Burned out on religion? Come to Me. Get away with Me and you'll recover your life. I'll show you how to take a real rest. Walk with Me and work with Me—watch how I do it. Learn the unforced rhythms of grace. I won't lay anything heavy or ill-fitting on you. Keep company with Me and you'll learn to live freely and lightly* (Matthew 11:28-30 MSG).

Hear the voice of God. Come away with Me. Recover your life. Take a real rest. Hear in the unforced rhythms a dance of Edenic delight.

There is a holy leisure that invites continual re-creation and friendship with God, people, and nature!

It gets even better! These cycles of one-year national vacations were setting the stage for a once-in-a-lifetime grand finale! After seven Sabbath years, God wanted His Jewish people to experience the lollapalooza of His joy: the *Year of Jubilee!*

On the fiftieth annual Day of Atonement, when every sin was covered and the Jews were "at one"—or Here-Now—with their loving God, shofars were to be blown from one end of Israel to the other heralding an unimaginable Heaven-on-earth experience.

God just took blessing to *a new level*. Proclaim liberty throughout the land! To everyone! Let the real party begin![6]

In Jubilee, everything lost was restored. Finances, relationships, and dignity were fully returned and repaired. For Israel it was an unconditional, universal rehabilitation. Jubilee returned every person's lifestyle to the "way it should be." Prisoners were released; those sold into slavery were set free from bondage. The ones who had lost their family inheritance got it back. The ones who were estranged were restored! The blessings of Abraham were reinstated.

Anyone who had messed up his life or any victims of setbacks and reversals got a new beginning, a fresh start. They got their lives back. This was not a stingy, you-had-better-shape-up, barely-get-by kind of reprieve. No! This was like a New Creation rolled out every 50 years—with lots and lots of supernatural grace and glory.

This Jubilee "commanded blessing" of God could have rocked the entire world once every 50 years! Israel would have taken its proper place as the global center for Delight Evangelism. Mount Zion would have been the joy of the whole earth! This is the personality of the Father!

With heartache, we see that Israel blindly turned away from this overflowing grace! Unbelief kept them from plunging into an ocean of joy. Disobedience robbed them of abundant life. They failed to enter the deep and full delights of their own national salvation.

Even today, our Father's unparalleled offer of supernatural blessing has not been rescinded. God keeps renewing the promise and setting the date as "Today."[7] Don't turn a deaf ear to the Here-Now delights of living in Jubilee blessing!

There is supernatural glory and blessing that is waiting for the people of God. The entire universe is poised and waiting with eager anticipation for the redeemed to enter and reveal the glories of their true identity.[8] All creation is longing for glorious liberty and grace that will renovate the entire universe. It's the restoration of all things, and it is connected to ceasing from our own works, entering into a true Sabbath.

> *There remains, then, a Sabbath-rest for the people of God; for anyone who enters God's rest also rests from his own work, just as God did from His* (Hebrews 4:9-10).

It remains. It's waiting for us. Today, Here-Now. While the Jubilee is unfulfilled on a universal level, it is completely accessible on a personal level.

Move in and live in continual bliss! It sounds like an oxymoron, but it's absolutely required that you expend every energy you have to throw yourself into that rest where all personal effort ends. The effort is not to please God, but to completely believe that God is pleased. He pleased Himself at the Cross. His gift and your personal future is a life of nonstop compassionate delight. If you enter into His rest, you have personally checkmated the world, the flesh, and the devil! You have moved into **love** and remained there. The blessings of God will flow through you into a desperate world as the rivers flowed out of Eden! You will supernaturally affect everything you touch.

You are the walking, talking, engraved invitation our Father has sent into the world to summon every creature to His Ultimate Party—the Wedding Supper of the Lamb. You have become the invitation of the Spirit, the Bride, and all those who hear. Your life calls out:

> … *"Come!"*

> *Whoever is thirsty, let him come; and whoever wishes, let him take the free gift of the water of life* (Revelation 22:17).

Endnotes

1. See Exodus 16:27.

2. See Exodus 31:17.

3. See Exodus 23:14-17.

4. See Luke 2.

5. See Leviticus 25:21 NKJV.

6. See Lev. 25:8-11.

7. See Hebrews 4:7 MSG.

8. See Romans 8:19-21.

Afterword

In these pages I've told some of my own story and hopefully inspired you to live intentionally in His grace. It has been a journey from darkness to light. I came as the prodigal son and was richly robed in the garments of salvation. As a newly restored prodigal, I danced with delight and beyond-belief joy at Father's feast thrown in my honor. I must confess that at times I became the older brother. I worked hard in the fields and was a faithful but unloving son, expecting others to work at least as hard. For moments and even seasons, I seemed to forget the music and festive joy of dancing in the sunny generosity of my Father's grace for all.

Don't worry, I have returned to the Party that never ends! I am making my home in the joy, becoming more and more like my Father. It's effortless.

We are living together in the At-One-Ment.

On that day you will realize that I am in My Father, and you are in Me, and I am in you (John 14:20).

That day is Today. Come on into the Party. Live *in* the land of love. No more commuter flights to misery.

There are many more stories I could tell, but I don't want to wear you out. I want to invite you to live in the fullness of God's great salvation.

Here are some final thoughts, beginning with some questions I ask myself when I catch myself leaving the Party:

1. Am I *"Here-Now?"*

   - Without worry or anxiety?

   - Without shame?

   - Without resentment or blame?

2. Is the radiant energy of God shining from my eyes?

   - Dripping from my words?

   - Governing how I hear?

   - Expressed in my actions?

3. Are my roots and foundation fully *in* supernatural love?

   - Free from personal agenda?

   - Free from judgment?

   - Free from corruption?

4. Am I complete, full, juicy, and fresh in the overflowing joy of Heaven?

   - Nutritious, fragrant, and bursting with Life?

   - Better than a good cup of coffee?

   - More delightful than a glass of fine wine?

5. Am I living in Jubilee, true rest, and playful celebration?

   - Taking a permanent break from my own efforts?

   - Living in the Father's House?

   - Experiencing commanded blessings?

Words are important. They capture and express the impulses of our hearts and minds. Jesus is the Word of God. Sometimes we lack vocabulary.

Here are some terms I find useful as I do a personal inventory of my emotional state. I ask myself: What am I experiencing? What am I radiating? What is my nonverbal message to the world around me?

Some good words: Pleasure, happiness, joy, glee, gladness, energy, rapture, elation, jubilation, triumph, exultation, exhilaration, exuberance, euphoria, enjoyment, felicity, joie de vivre, jouissance, contentment, satisfaction, cheerfulness, merriment, gaiety, joviality, good spirits, lightheartedness, well-being, delight, bliss, ecstasy!

Remember! Against such things there is no law…

Finally…

And so we know and rely on the love God has for us.

God is love.

Whoever lives in love lives in God,

and God in him (1 John 4:16)!

Ministry Page

Have you been impacted by *Glow in the Dark?*

Would you like more?

Is freedom calling to you?

You can learn more about the teaching
materials and ministries of

Charles and Anne Stock

by visiting

http://www.lcmi.org/glow

For further contact please contact
Life Center Ministries International
(717) 232-9006

Additional copies of this book and other
book titles from DESTINY IMAGE are
available at your local bookstore.

Call toll-free: 1-800-722-6774.

Send a request for a catalog to:

Destiny Image® Publishers, Inc.

P.O. Box 310
Shippensburg, PA 17257-0310

*"Speaking to the Purposes of God for This
Generation and for the Generations to Come."*

**For a complete list of our titles,
visit us at www.destinyimage.com.**